I0815084

SHARKS

by Marne Ventura

Early Encyclopedias

An Imprint of Abdo Reference
abdobooks.com

abdobooks.com

Published by Abdo Reference, a division of ABDO, PO Box 398166, Minneapolis, Minnesota 55439.

Printed in the United States of America, North Mankato, Minnesota.
102022
012023

Editor: Katharine Hale
Series Designers: Candice Keimig, Joshua Olson

Library of Congress Control Number: 2022940691

Publisher's Cataloging-in-Publication Data

Names: Ventura, Marne, author.
Title: Sharks / by Marne Ventura
Description: Minneapolis, Minnesota: Abdo Publishing, 2023 | Series: Early animal encyclopedias | Includes online resources and index.
Identifiers: ISBN 9781098290443 (lib. bdg.) | ISBN 9781098275761 (ebook)
Subjects: LCSH: Sharks--Juvenile literature. | Sharks--Behavior--Juvenile literature. | Zoology--Juvenile literature. | Encyclopedias and dictionaries--Juvenile literature.
Classification: DDC 597.3--dc23

CONTENTS

What Are Sharks?

Sharks are fish. A shark's skeleton is made of cartilage instead of bone. This helps sharks float. Sharks breathe through gills. Their skin is made of tiny, sharp scales. Sharks have good eyesight and hearing. They also have a good sense of smell.

There are more than 500 different shark species. They range in size from less than 7 inches (18 cm) to more than 55 feet (17 m) long. Most sharks are gray. But they can be many other colors. Some have spots or stripes.

Sharks eat plankton, shellfish, fish, and ocean mammals such as seals. Sharks bite off pieces of their food. They swallow each piece whole. Sharks have many teeth. When a shark loses a tooth, a new one takes its place.

Sharks have lived in Earth's oceans for more than 400 million years. Only a few species of

sharks will bite humans. When they do, it is usually because they are confused or afraid.

AUSTRALIAN SWELLSHARK

(*Cephaloscyllium laticeps*)

The Australian swellshark can also be called the draughtboard shark, nutcracker shark, or sleepy joe.

Appearance

Australian swellsharks have short, wide, round heads. Their eyes are cat-like. Their bodies are brown or gray. They are covered with dark and light spots. At birth, they are about the size of a cell phone. Most adults grow to be as long as a baseball bat.

Behavior

Swellsharks are not very active. They move more during the night than the day. Swellsharks eat small fish, crustaceans, shrimp, and squid. A swellshark can fill its stomach with air or water. This makes the shark look bigger. Predators might be scared away.

3.3 to 4.9 feet
(1 to 1.5 m)

Weight:
Weight not documented

Range

Australian swellsharks live in shallow water. They are often found near southeastern Australia. They live near rocky and sandy areas of the ocean floor.

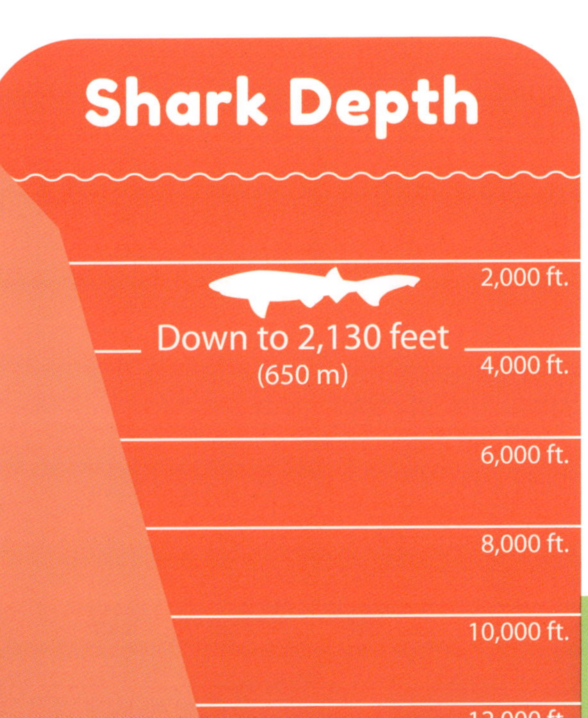

BASKING SHARK

(*Cetorhinus maximus*)

Basking sharks swim very slowly.

Appearance

Basking sharks are the second-largest living fish. Most are as long as a school bus. They can weigh as much as two cars. They are grayish brown or black.

Behavior

Basking sharks often float near the surface of the water.

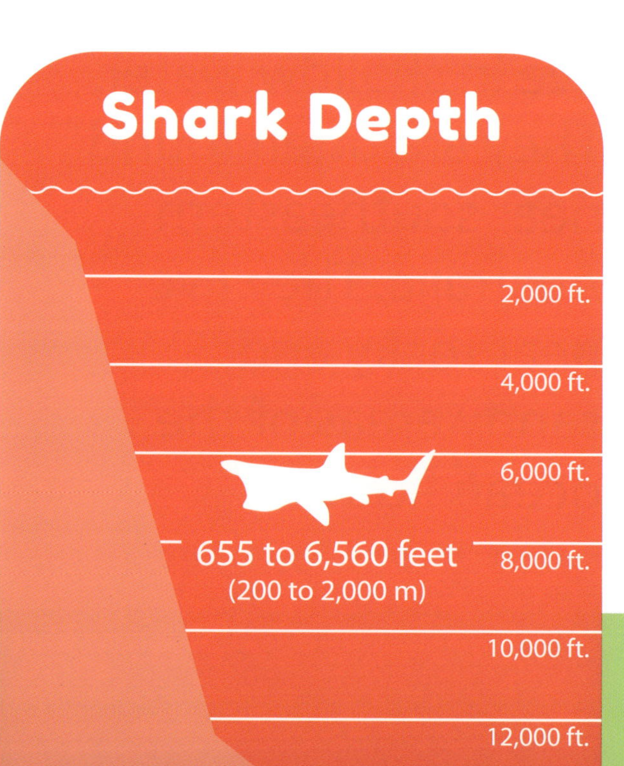

They have hairs called gill rakers on the insides of their mouths. To eat, a basking shark opens its mouth to let water in. The gill rakers separate tiny ocean animals from the water. These animals will go to the shark's stomach. The extra water goes out through the gills.

Range

Basking sharks live mostly along the coasts of the Atlantic and Pacific Oceans. They have been seen near the Hawaiian Islands. They stay in areas where the weather is mild.

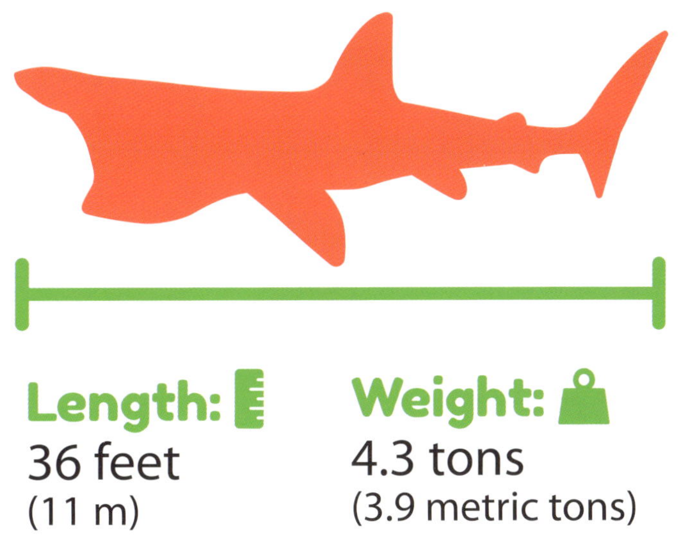

Length:
36 feet
(11 m)

Weight:
4.3 tons
(3.9 metric tons)

BIGEYE THRESHER SHARK

(*Alopias superciliosus*)

Bigeye threshers are not considered harmful to humans.

Appearance

Bigeye thresher sharks have large eyes. They also have huge tail fins. The tail fin can be as long as the shark's body.

Behavior

These sharks stay near the ocean surface at night.

Length: 11 to 16 feet (3.5 to 4.9 m)

Weight: Up to 802 pounds (364 kg)

During the day, they dive down to hunt. They stun fish and squid by hitting them with their big tail fins. This makes it easier to catch and eat the prey. Bigeye threshers can also make their bodies get warmer than the ocean water. This helps them stay in deep or cold water while hunting.

Range

Bigeye thresher sharks live in the Atlantic Ocean. They stay near the equator. The weather there is warm. These sharks are also found in the Mediterranean Sea.

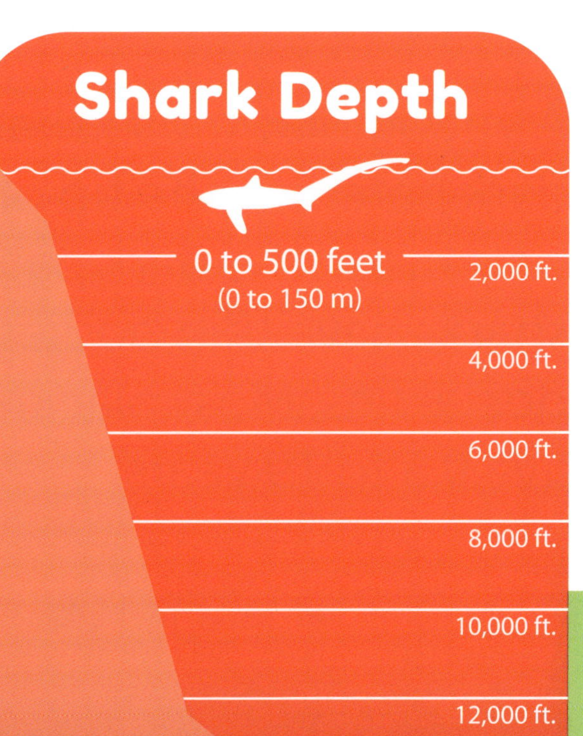

BLACKNOSE SHARK

(*Carcharhinus acronotus*)

Blacknose sharks can be eaten by larger sharks.

Appearance

A young blacknose shark has a dark patch on the tip of its snout. As the shark gets older, the dark patch fades away. These sharks have thin bodies. They have two small dorsal fins. Most blacknose sharks are gray. They live 9.5 to 19 years.

Behavior

Blacknose sharks swim quickly. They eat small fish and octopuses. When afraid, a Blacknose shark will arch its back, raise its head, and lower its tail. This is called a defensive display.

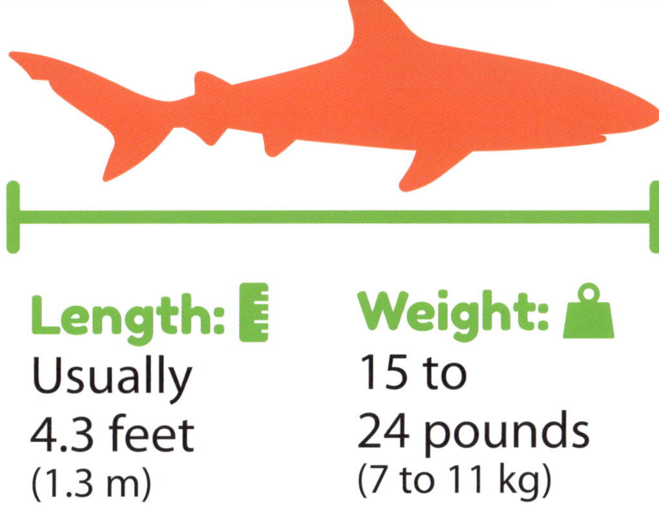

Range

This shark lives in warm water. It can be seen along the coast of the western Atlantic Ocean. Young sharks stay in shallow water. Adults are found in deeper water.

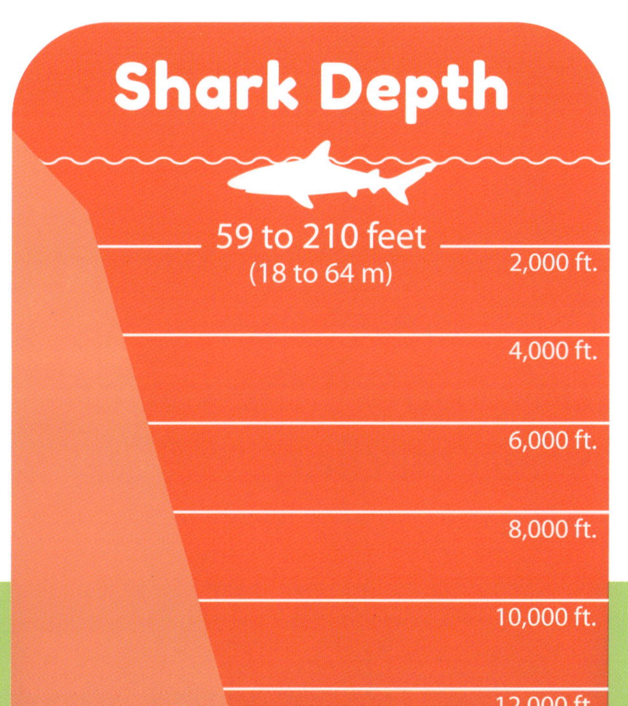

BLACKTIP REEF SHARK

(*Carcharhinus melanopterus*)

Appearance

Blacktip reef sharks have dark-gray bodies. Their undersides are white. They have black tips on their fins. This is where they get their name. Their snouts are short and blunt. Their teeth are serrated like the edge of a saw. Blacktip reef sharks can grow to be as long as an adult's bicycle.

Behavior

Blacktip reef sharks swim in groups called schools. These sharks eat reef fish and small shellfish. They sometimes jump out of the water when feeding.

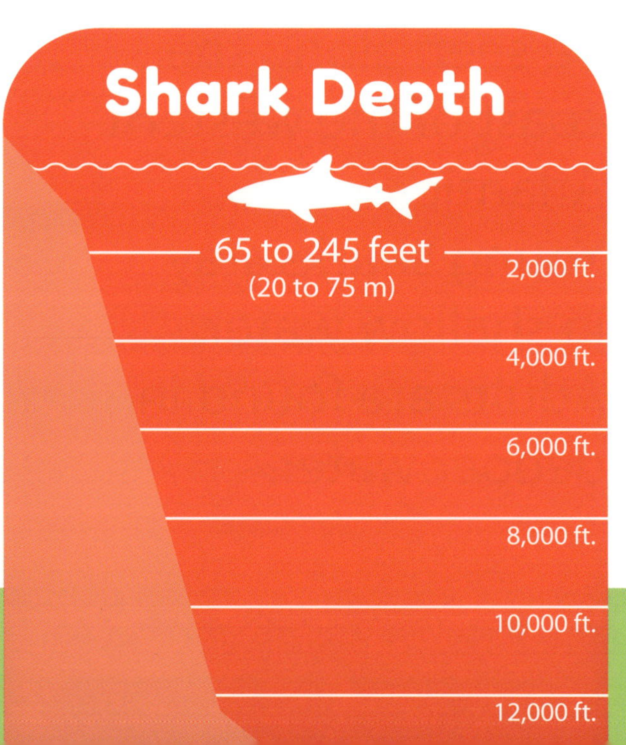

Blacktip reef sharks swim among coral reefs.

Range

Blacktip reef sharks live near reefs where the sea is shallow. They are found on the coast of the Pacific Ocean near Thailand, Japan, and northern Australia. They also live in the Indian Ocean from South Africa to the Red Sea.

Length: Up to 6.6 feet (2 m)

Weight: Up to 30 pounds (14 kg)

BLACKTIP SHARK

(*Carcharhinus limbatus*)

Appearance

The blacktip shark is named for its fins, which have black tips. Its back is dark gray or brown. Its underside is white. It has a torpedo-shaped body. Blacktip sharks can weigh as much as a small refrigerator.

Behavior

Sometimes blacktip sharks jump out of the water. They turn themselves around in the air. Then they splash into the water on their backs. Scientists think this

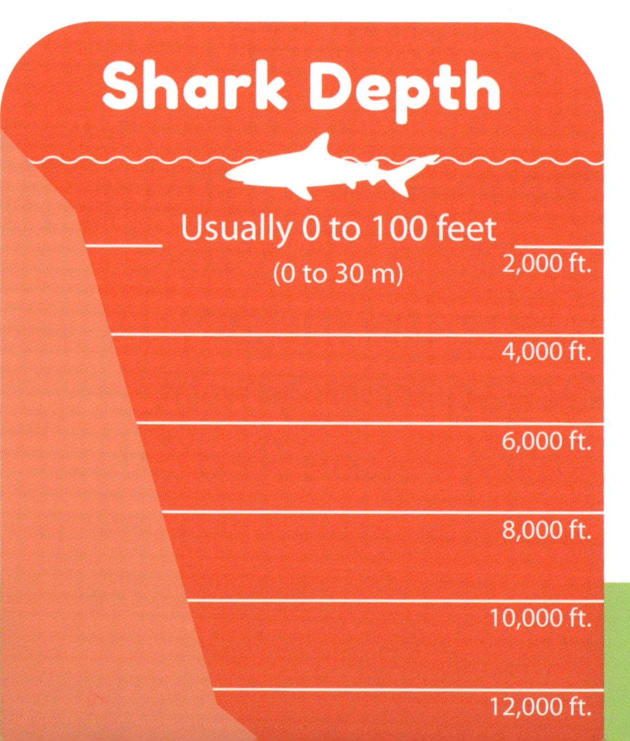

helps the shark catch its prey. The sharks surprise their prey by moving fast. Blacktip sharks eat skates, rays, shellfish, and other fish.

Length: Up to 8 feet (2.4 m)

Weight: 66 to 220 pounds (30 to 100 kg)

Range

Blacktip sharks are found around the world. They usually swim near the coast. They feed in bays and near coral reefs where the water is shallow.

Blacktip sharks can move quickly through the water.

BLUE SHARK

(Prionace glauca)

Appearance

Blue sharks have slim bodies. Their snouts are cone shaped. The shark has a blue back. Its underside is white. A blue shark's coloring helps it hide from predators and prey. The dark side blends in with the deep sea. The light side blends in with the sunny surface. This means the shark can sneak up on its prey from above and below.

Length: Up to 13 feet (4 m)

Weight: Up to 530 pounds (240 kg)

Behavior

Blue sharks are curious. They swim up to divers to find food. They do not normally

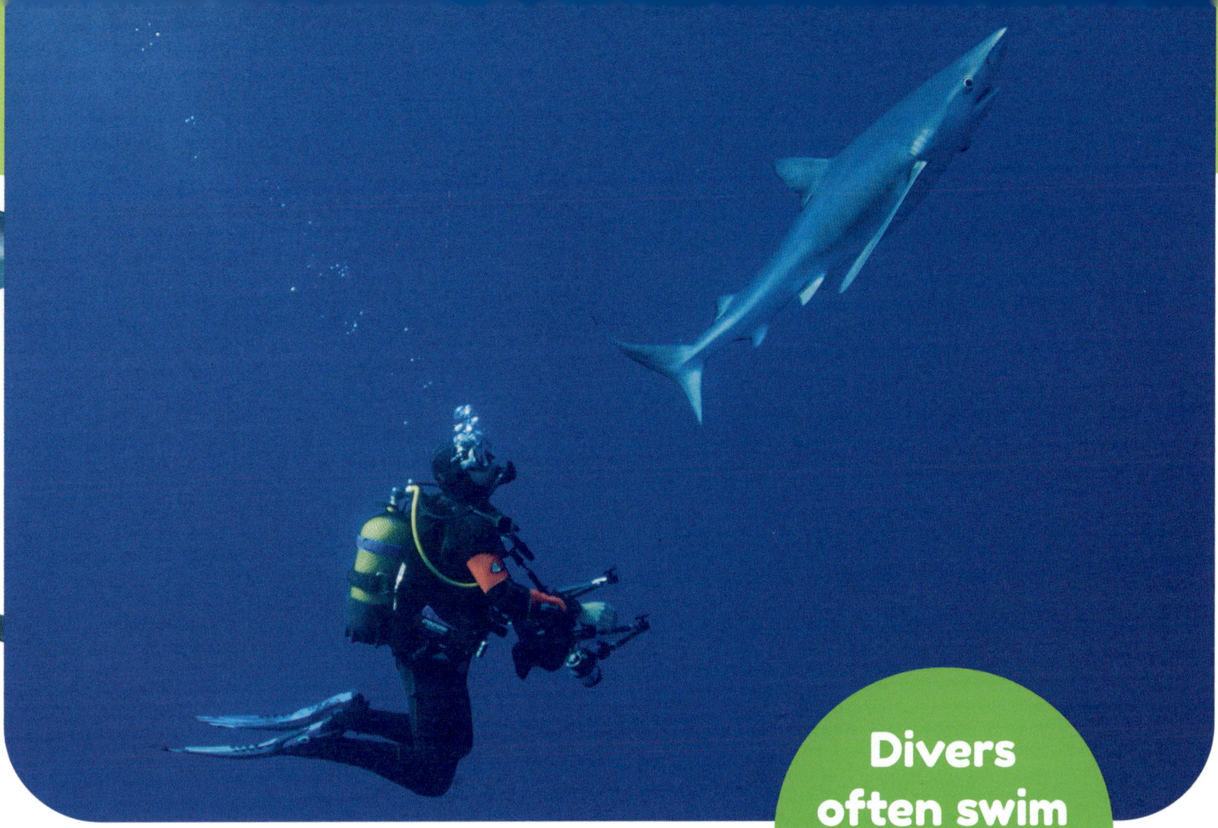

Divers often swim near blue sharks.

attack humans. Blue sharks feed on small fish and squid. They eat at night.

Range

Blue sharks are found around the world. They prefer the open sea. They rarely swim near the shore.

Shark Depth

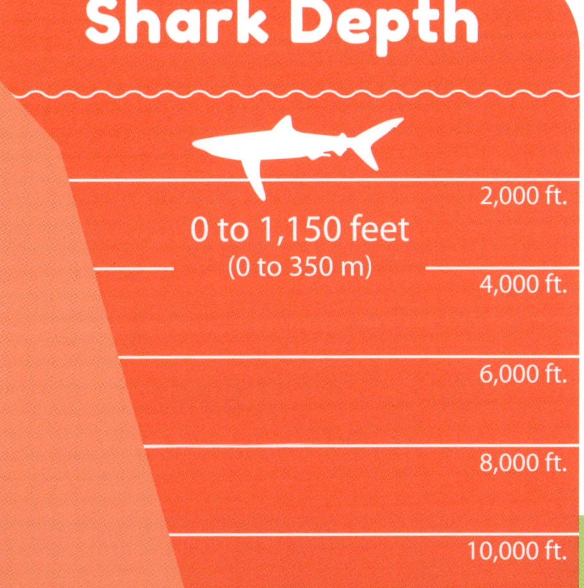

BLUNTNOSE SIXGILL SHARK

(*Hexanchus griseus*)

Appearance

The bluntnose sixgill shark is one of the world's largest sharks. It has six wide teeth on each side of its lower jaw. These teeth create a saw-like shape. There are serrated teeth on each side of its upper jaw. Experts think this shark catches prey in its jaws. Then it moves its head back and forth like a saw to take a bite.

Behavior

Bluntnose sixgill sharks are slow, strong swimmers. They rest on the ocean floor during the day. They swim

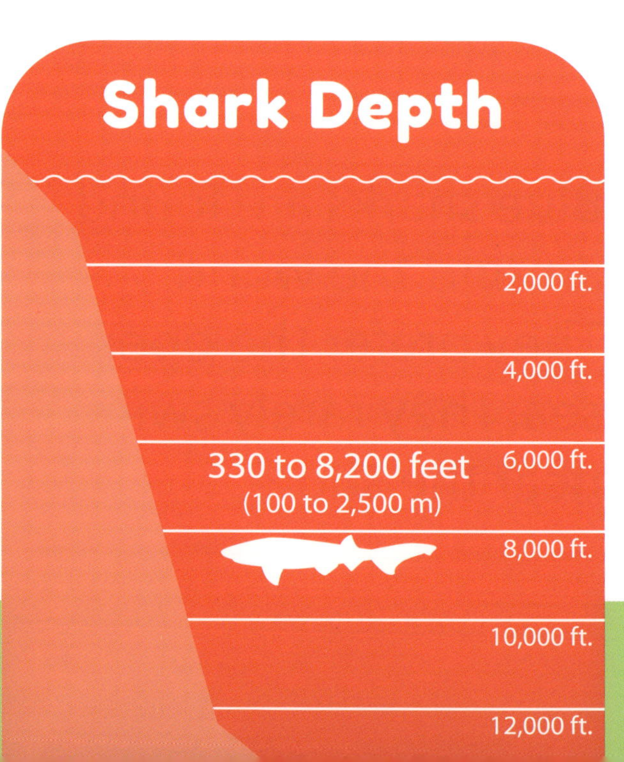

Bluntnose sixgill sharks grab and hold fish with their sharp teeth.

close to the surface of the water at night.

Range

Bluntnose sixgill sharks are found around the world. They swim in the Pacific, Atlantic, and Indian Oceans. They are also found in the Mediterranean Sea.

Length:
Up to 16 feet
(4.8 m)

Weight:
Up to 1,300 pounds
(590 kg)

BONNETHEAD SHARK

(*Sphyrna tiburo*)

Appearance

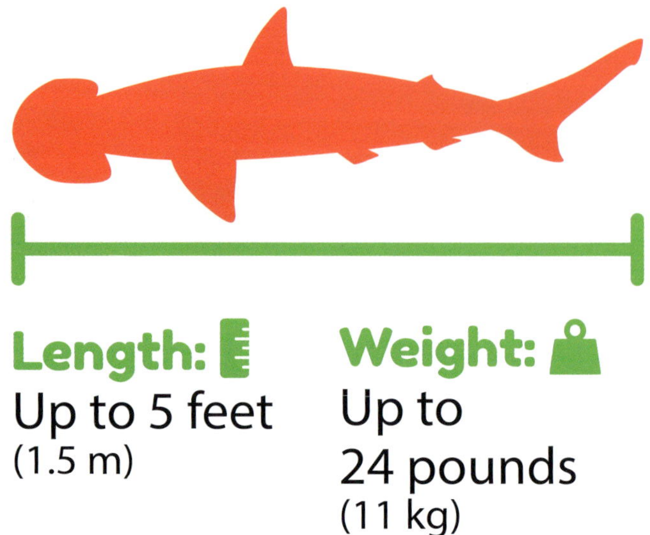

Length: Up to 5 feet (1.5 m)

Weight: Up to 24 pounds (11 kg)

The bonnethead shark has a wide, flat head. Its head looks like the scoop of a shovel. Its eyes are at the sides of its head. This shark is the smallest type of hammerhead shark. Its back can be gray or brown. Its underside is white. Sometimes it has dark spots on its sides.

Behavior

Bonnethead sharks feed on small fish, crabs, shrimp, and octopuses. Bonnetheads create a special fluid. They release it into the water. Experts think

the bonnethead uses the fluid to tell other bonnetheads that it is near.

The head shape of bonnetheads gives them a wide field of vision.

Range

Bonnethead sharks swim in the western Atlantic Ocean, the Caribbean Sea, and the Pacific Ocean. They stay on sandy bottoms near the shore. They also like coral reefs and bays.

Shark Depth

30 to 260 feet
(10 to 80 m)

2,000 ft.
4,000 ft.
6,000 ft.
8,000 ft.
10,000 ft.
12,000 ft.

BROWNBANDED BAMBOO SHARK

(*Chiloscyllium punctatum*)

Appearance

The brownbanded bamboo shark is long and thin with a rounded snout. Young sharks have dark stripes and spots. The color and pattern of their skin makes them hard to see on the ocean floor. This is called camouflage. Camouflage helps them hide from predators. As the

Length: Up to 3.4 feet (1 m)

Weight: Up to 10 pounds (4.6 kg)

sharks age, they turn light brown. The pattern fades.

The color of the brownbanded bamboo shark grows duller as it gets older.

Behavior

Brownbanded bamboo sharks feed on fish, crabs, and shrimp. They search for food by digging in the sand. They stay near coral reefs on the sandy ocean floor. They swim alone.

Range

These sharks live near the shore. They swim in oceans near India, Japan, and the Philippines. They are also found near northern Australia.

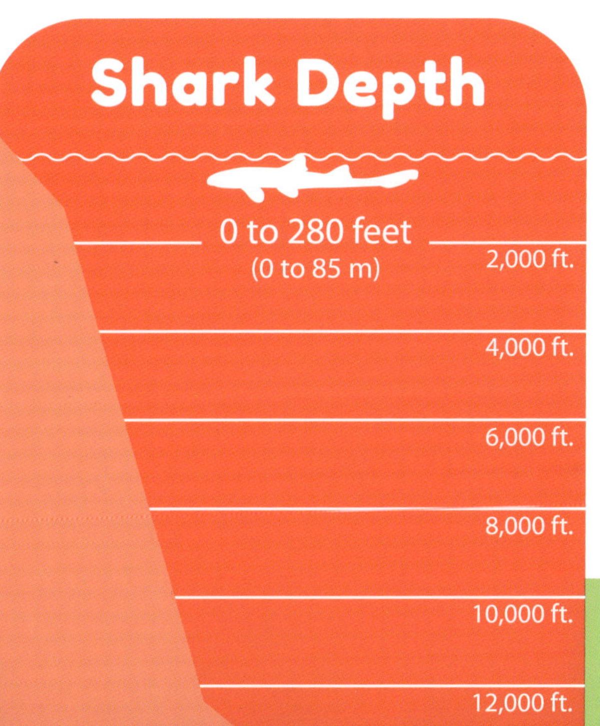

BULL SHARK

(*Carcharhinus leucas*)

Appearance

The bull shark has a thick body. Its snout is short and blunt. Bull sharks are gray with white undersides. They have sharp teeth. They also have strong jaws.

Behavior

The bull shark is fierce. It feeds mostly on fish. It will also eat smaller sharks, skates, birds, and mammals. Like a bull, it attacks its prey with a headbutt. It grabs prey with its teeth. Then it swings its head from side to side to pull off a piece to eat.

Length: Usually around 10 feet (3 m)

Weight: Usually 210 to 245 pounds (95 to 111 kg)

The bull shark's coloring helps it blend in with the water around it.

Range

Bull sharks are found near the shore in shallow water. They swim in tropical oceans around the world. They have also been found in freshwater rivers such as the Amazon.

Shark Depth

Usually 0 to 100 feet
(0 to 30 m)

2,000 ft.
4,000 ft.
6,000 ft.
8,000 ft.
10,000 ft.
12,000 ft.

CARIBBEAN REEF SHARK

(*Carcharhinus perezi*)

Appearance

The Caribbean reef shark is dark gray or grayish brown. It has a lighter underside. Its snout is short and round. Its eyes are large. Caribbean reef sharks can grow to be about as long as a ping-pong table.

Behavior

Caribbean reef sharks eat large fish and squid. They snap their jaws quickly to catch their prey in the corners of their mouths. Caribbean reef sharks can be fierce around food. If threatened, the shark may lower its tail. It quickly changes direction.

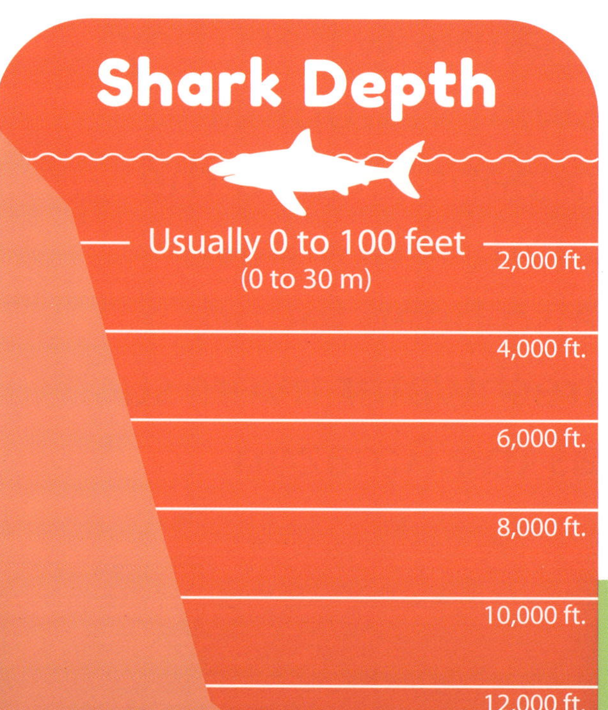

Caribbean reef sharks rarely attack people.

Range

The Caribbean reef shark lives in the Caribbean Sea. It is also found off the coasts of North, Central, and South America. It swims near coral reefs. It stays in shallow waters.

Length: Up to 9.8 feet (3 m)

Weight: Up to 155 pounds (70 kg)

CARIBBEAN SHARPNOSE SHARK

(*Rhizoprionodon porosus*)

Appearance

The Caribbean sharpnose shark has a small, slender body. Its snout is long. Its back is brown or grayish brown. Its underside is white. Sometimes it has white spots along its sides. Caribbean sharpnose sharks live for about eight years.

Behavior

Caribbean sharpnose sharks eat small fish, squid, crabs, and shrimp. They stay close to the shoreline. They also swim in bays. Sometimes they are found in rivers.

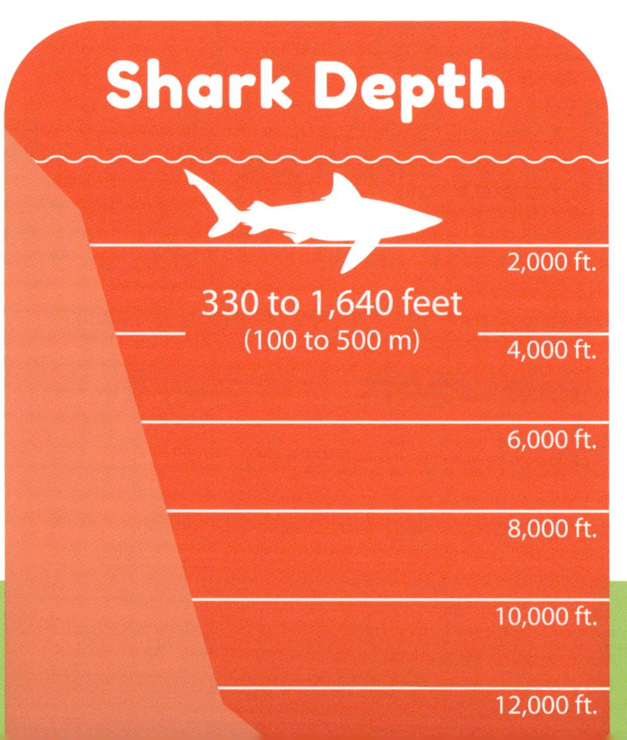

Like many sharks, the Caribbean sharpnose has a light-colored underside.

If human divers come near, these sharks will swim away to avoid contact. Caribbean sharpnose sharks give birth to live young.

Range

The Caribbean sharpnose shark lives in the Caribbean Sea. It can be found near the Bahamas. It also swims along the northeastern coast of South America.

Length: Usually 2.6 feet (0.8 m)

Weight: Up to 16.5 pounds (7.5 kg)

CHAIN DOGFISH SHARK

(*Scyliorhinus retifer*)

Appearance

The chain dogfish shark is small and thin. Its body is brownish yellow. The pattern on its back looks like a black chain.

Behavior

The pattern on the chain dogfish shark serves as camouflage. The shark's dark and light colors blend in with the rocks and sand. This makes it hard for predators to see the shark. Chain dogfish sharks stay in rocky areas near the ocean floor. They eat small fish, squid, ocean worms, and crustaceans.

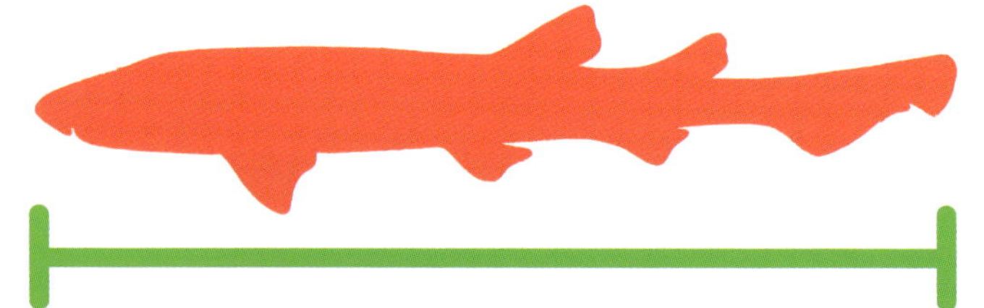

Length:
16 to
18 inches
(41 to 45 cm)

Weight:
11 to
13 ounces
(300 to 380 g)

The chain dogfish shark swims along the ocean floor.

Range

Chain dogfish sharks are found on the eastern coast of the United States. They live in the western Atlantic Ocean. These sharks are also found in the Gulf of Mexico and the Caribbean Sea.

Shark Depth

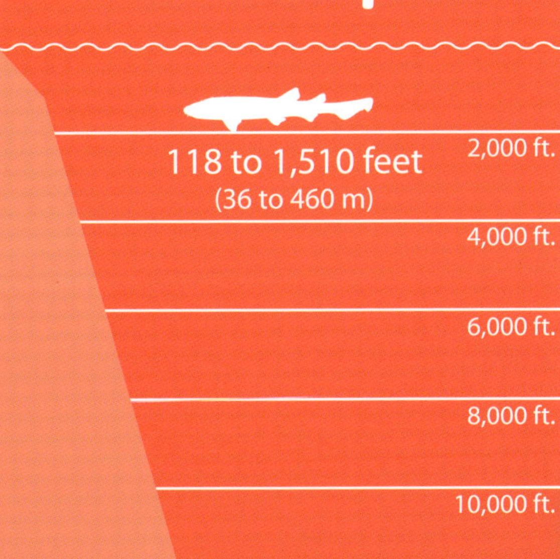

COMMON ANGELSHARK

(Squatina squatina)

The common angelshark is hard to spot when it lies on the ocean floor.

Appearance

The common angelshark is flat. It looks like a ray or a skate. It has barbels near its snout. Barbels look like thick whiskers. They help the shark smell its prey. Common angelsharks can be white, gray, brown, or black. These colors help them blend in with the ocean floor. This is where these sharks live.

Length: Usually 4.9 feet (1.5 m)

Weight: Up to 175 pounds (80 kg)

Behavior

Common angelsharks bury themselves in sand. This helps them hide. They hunt for food at night. A common angelshark lies still on the ocean floor. Then prey swims by. The shark springs up to attack. These sharks eat fish, skates, and crustaceans.

Range

Common angelsharks are found in the Mediterranean Sea. They also live in the eastern Atlantic Ocean. Some hide out in areas where a river meets the ocean.

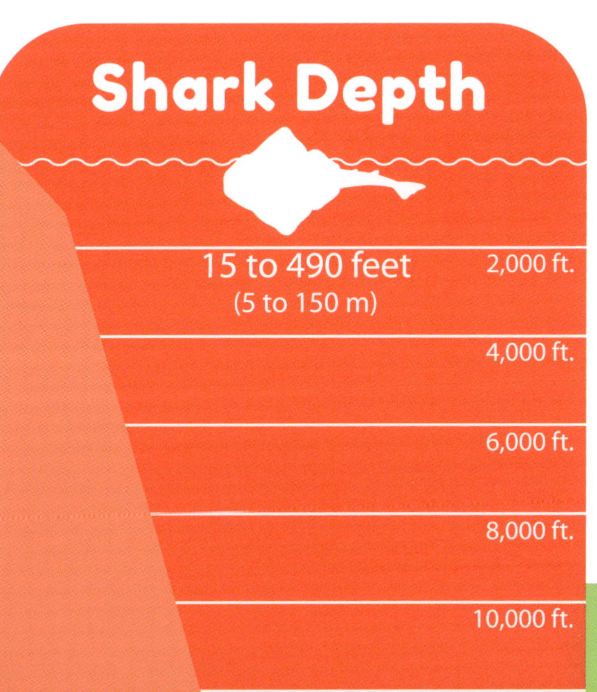

COMMON SAWSHARK

(*Pristiophorus cirratus*)

Appearance

The common sawshark has a long, flat snout with long barbels. The snout has 19 to 25 teeth on each side. The common sawshark's body is snake-like. Its back is gray or brown. Its belly is white. Two brown stripes run along the top of the snout.

Behavior

Common sawsharks travel in schools. They use their barbels to sense what is around them. They stun their prey by hitting them with their snouts. This knocks out the prey. The sharks feed on fish, shrimp, small squid, and crustaceans.

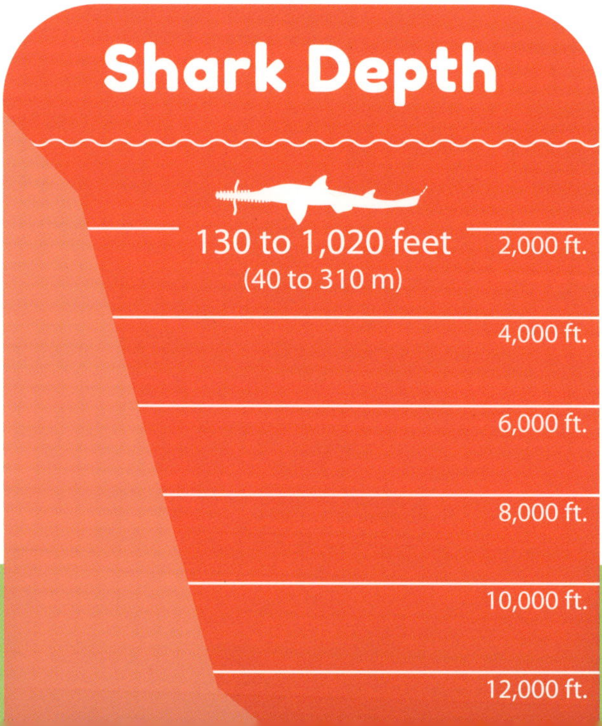

Shark Depth

130 to 1,020 feet
(40 to 310 m)

2,000 ft.
4,000 ft.
6,000 ft.
8,000 ft.
10,000 ft.
12,000 ft.

The common sawshark uses its unique snout for hunting.

Range

Common sawsharks are found in Australia. They range from New South Wales to southwestern Western Australia. They swim near the coast.

Length: Up to 4.9 feet (1.5 m)

Weight: Up to 19 pounds (8.5 kg)

COMMON SMOOTH-HOUND SHARK

(*Mustelus mustelus*)

Appearance

The common smooth-hound shark is large and thin. It has a short head and snout. It is gray or brown with a white underside. Sometimes it has dark spots. Males grow to 3.6 feet (1.1 m) long. Females grow to 5.4 feet (1.6 m) long.

Behavior

The common smooth-hound shark eats crustaceans and fish. Common smooth-hound sharks sometimes gather together. This behavior is similar to that of a pack

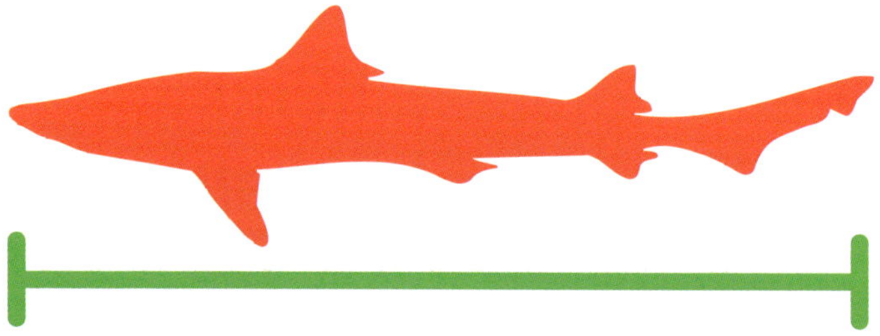

Length: Up to 3.6 to 5.4 feet (1.1 to 1.6 m)

Weight: Weight not documented

The skin of a common smooth-hound shark under a microscope

of wild dogs. That is where the shark got its name.

Range

Common smooth-hound sharks are found in the eastern Atlantic Ocean. They also swim in the Mediterranean Sea and the Indian Ocean. They usually stay in shallow waters. But they can live at depths of 1,150 feet (350 m) or more.

Shark Depth

Usually 15 to 165 feet
(5 to 50 m)

2,000 ft.
4,000 ft.
6,000 ft.
8,000 ft.
10,000 ft.
12,000 ft.

COMMON THRESHER SHARK

(*Alopias vulpinus*)

Appearance

Common thresher sharks are brown, gray, bluish gray, or black. Their undersides are white. Their fins are black. Sometimes they have white dots on the tips of their fins. The upper part of the tail fin is long. It can be as long as half of the shark's body length.

Behavior

Common thresher sharks eat fish, squid, and seabirds. They use their long upper tails like whips. They hit their prey to stun it before eating it.

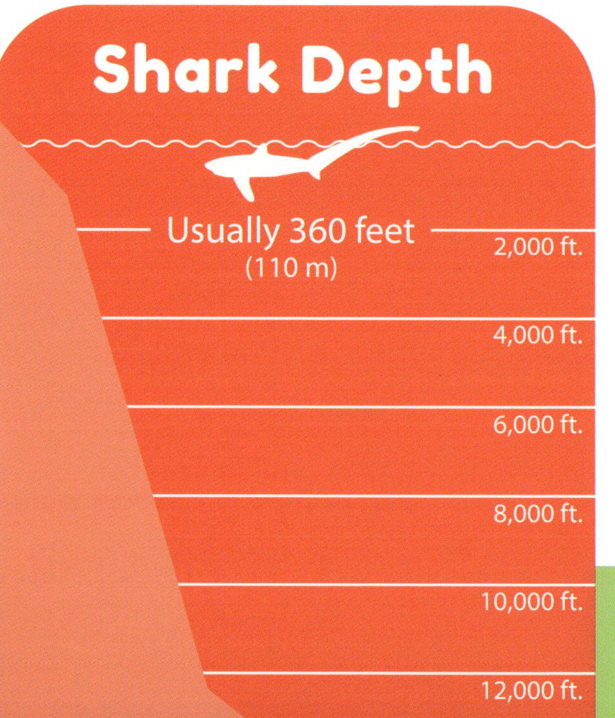

Common thresher sharks sometimes leap out of the water.

Range

Common thresher sharks are found around the world where water is warm. They swim in the Atlantic Ocean between Newfoundland and Cuba. They are also found in the north Pacific Ocean near North America and Asia.

Length:
5 to 20 feet
(1.6 to 6 m)

Weight:
Up to 1,100 pounds
(500 kg)

COOKIECUTTER SHARK

(*Isistius brasiliensis*)

Appearance

Cookiecutter sharks are small and tube shaped. Their snouts are short and round. They have big lips. They are gray or grayish brown. They have a dark stripe around their throats.

Behavior

Cookiecutter sharks are named for the way they feed. A cookiecutter shark attracts prey to its underside by giving off a glowing light. The light looks like a

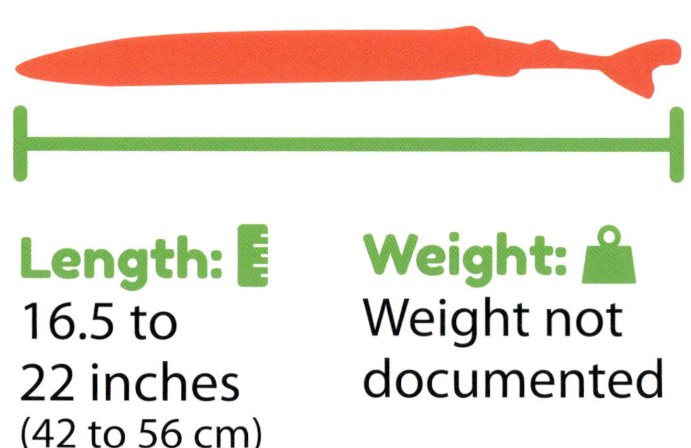

Length: 16.5 to 22 inches (42 to 56 cm)

Weight: Weight not documented

A bite wound from a cookiecutter shark on a yellowfin tuna.

small fish in the deep sea. When prey gets near, the cookiecutter shark bites and sucks on the prey. It removes a round piece. This process is similar to using a cookie cutter on dough.

Range

These sharks live near islands in tropical waters. They live in the Atlantic, southern Indian, and Pacific Oceans. Experts think they go to the ocean's surface at night.

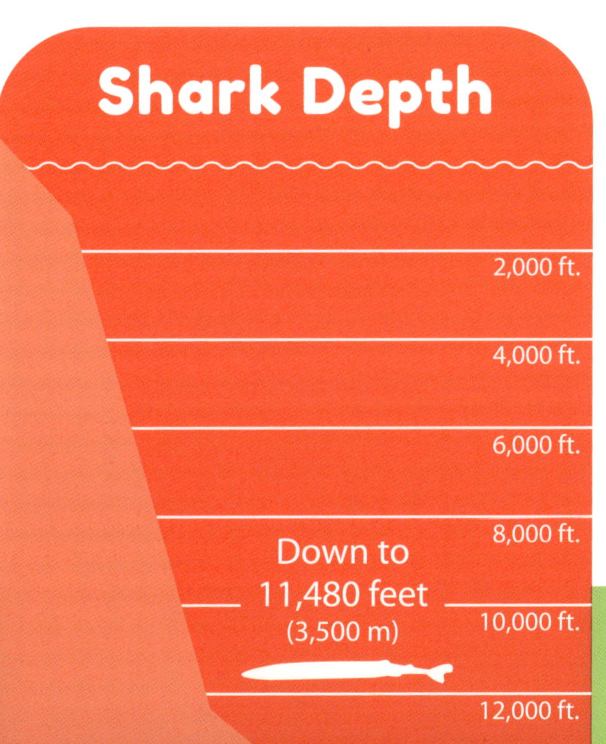

DUSKY SHARK

(*Carcharhinus obscurus*)

Appearance

The dusky shark gets its name from the dark-colored tips on its fins. It has a short, broad, round snout. It has a gray or blue-gray back and a white belly. The dusky shark's teeth are serrated. The upper teeth are wide. The lower teeth are narrow. Dusky sharks can live up to 50 years.

Behavior

Dusky sharks feed on fish, sharks, rays, and shellfish. They hunt on the ocean floor. They migrate to warm water in cold seasons and cooler water in warm seasons.

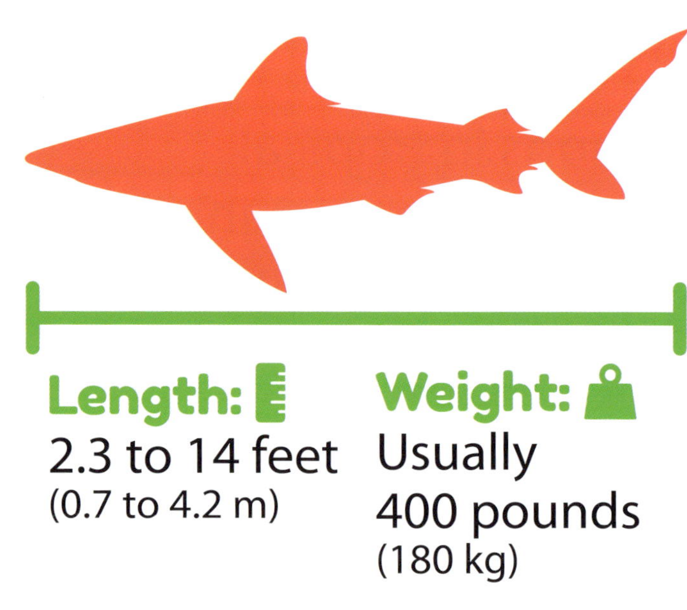

A dusky shark swims through a huge school of sardines.

Range

Dusky sharks are found where the weather is warm. They live along coasts in the Pacific, Atlantic, and Indian Oceans. They are also found in the Gulf of Mexico and Mediterranean Sea.

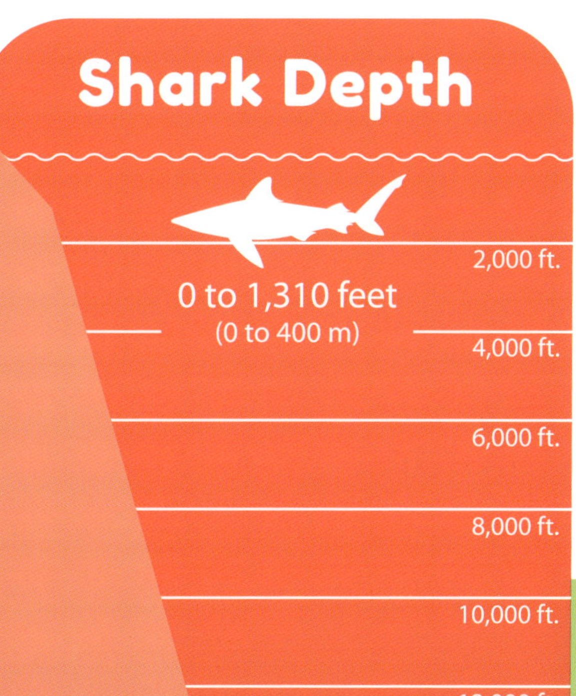

FRILLED SHARK

(*Chlamydoselachus anguineus*)

Appearance

The frilled shark is named for its gill slits. The ruffled gill slits look like frills. The frilled shark has a long, flattened body like an eel's. This shark can be longer than a twin-size bed. It has a dark-brown or gray back. Its underside is lighter.

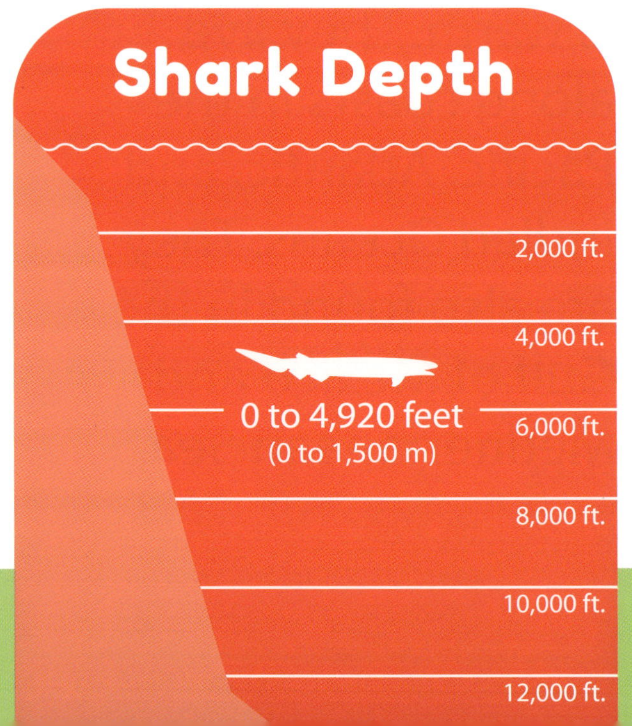

Behavior

Frilled sharks swim very slowly. They feed on squid, fish, and other sharks. To surprise its prey, a frilled shark may curve its body like a spring. Then it lunges forward and strikes like a snake. Frilled sharks often swallow their prey whole. Some scientists think frilled sharks use their large, white teeth to lure in prey.

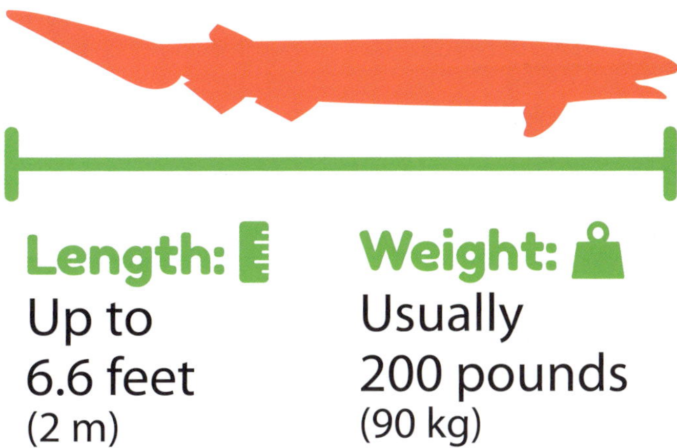

Length: Up to 6.6 feet (2 m)

Weight: Usually 200 pounds (90 kg)

Frilled sharks have a total of 300 teeth.

Range

Frilled sharks live in deep water. But they sometimes swim up to the surface. They can be found worldwide.

GOBLIN SHARK

(*Mitsukurina owstoni*)

The goblin shark extends its jaws when it is time to feed.

Appearance

The goblin shark is named for the spooky way it looks. It has a long snout that sticks out over its mouth. The mouth is lined with long, pointy teeth. The shark's flabby skin is pink, purple, or gray. The fins are blue.

Length: Up to 20 feet (6.2 m)

Weight: 330 to 460 pounds (150 to 210 kg)

Behavior

A goblin shark can stretch its mouth out to the end of its snout. This helps it catch and eat fish, squid, and crustaceans. The goblin shark moves its jaws forward faster than any other shark species when it is feeding.

Range

Goblin sharks are found on the ocean floor. They swim in the Pacific, Atlantic, and Indian Oceans. They can be found around the southern and southeastern coasts of Australia.

Shark Depth

GRAY REEF SHARK

(*Carcharhinus amblyrhynchos*)

Appearance

Gray reef sharks have dark-gray or bronze backs. Their undersides are white. Their fin bottoms have black tips. Gray reef sharks live for about 25 years.

Behavior

Gray reef sharks feed on fish, squid, crabs, and shrimp. This shark is curious. It will swim up to human divers. If it does not feel threatened, it swims away. If it senses a threat, it acts fierce. It wags its head and tail back and forth. It arches its

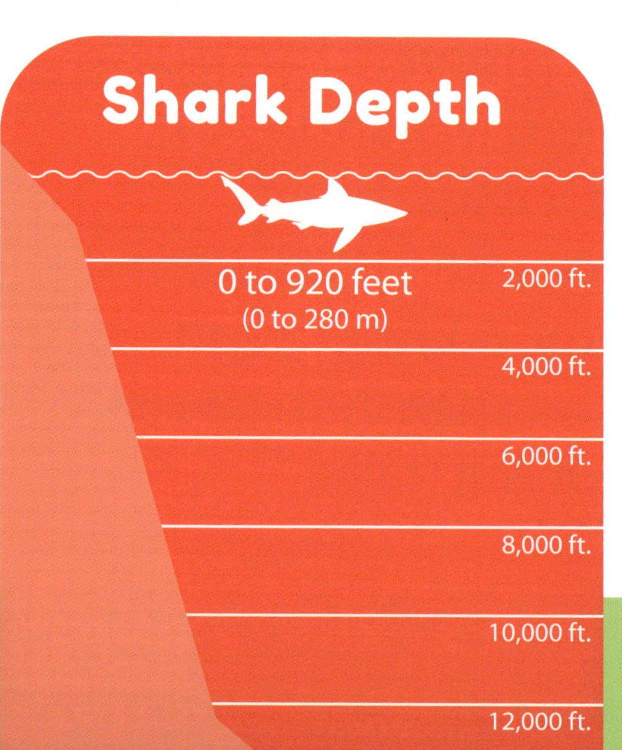

Gray reef sharks sometimes swim together in large groups.

back and lifts its head. It swims in a spiral or a loop. Then it attacks at high speed.

Range

Gray reef sharks are found in coral reefs and coastal areas. They live in the Indo-Pacific region. They are also found in the Red Sea.

Length: Up to around 6.2 feet (1.9 m)

Weight: Up to 75 pounds (34 kg)

GREAT HAMMERHEAD SHARK

(*Sphyrna mokarran*)

Appearance

The great hammerhead shark is the largest of the hammerhead sharks. Hammerheads are famous for the shape of their snouts. The great hammerhead's snout is wide and rectangular. It looks like the head of a hammer. The shark's eyes and nostrils are at each end of the snout. The shark has long, sharp teeth. These sharks have dark gray-brown backs. Their undersides are light gray.

Behavior

These sharks eat rays, skates, fish, and crustaceans. They pin their prey down with their snouts. Then they bite off pieces of the prey

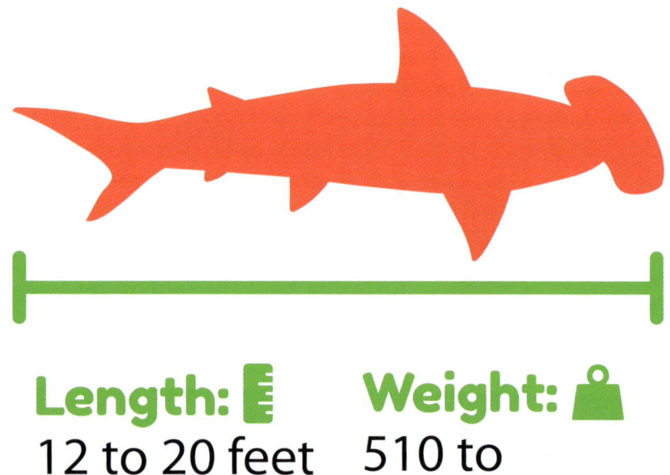

Length:
12 to 20 feet
(3.7 to 6.1 m)

Weight:
510 to 991 pounds
(230 to 450 kg)

to eat. Great hammerheads usually hunt at sunset.

Adult great hammerheads have no major predators.

Range

Great hammerheads are found around the world in tropical seas. They swim in shallow waters. They migrate long distances. Great hammerheads usually swim alone.

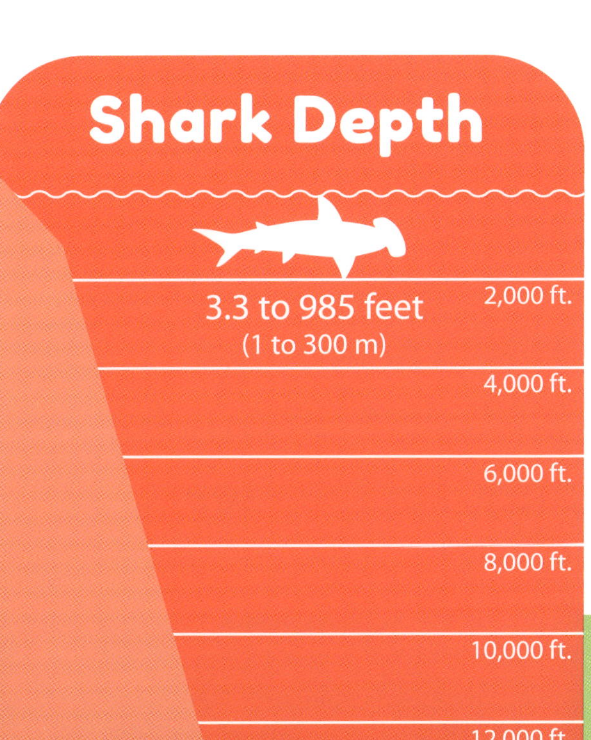

GREAT WHITE SHARK

(*Carcharodon carcharias*)

Appearance

The world's largest hunting, meat-eating fish is the great white shark. It has 300 teeth. Its huge body is torpedo shaped.

Behavior

A great white shark cruises through the water. Then it bursts into a high-speed chase after its prey. It often leaps out of the water to catch prey. Great white sharks sometimes bite humans who are in the ocean. Experts think the sharks confuse humans for prey, such as seals.

Length: Up to 21 feet (6.4 m)

Weight: Up to 3.3 tons (3 metric tons)

A great white shark will usually bite a human only once before swimming away.

Range

Great white sharks have a wide range. They are found in the Atlantic, Pacific, and Indian Oceans. They sometimes are found in the Mediterranean Sea. Some travel far out to sea. But most stay near the coast. Great whites stay in areas with lots of prey.

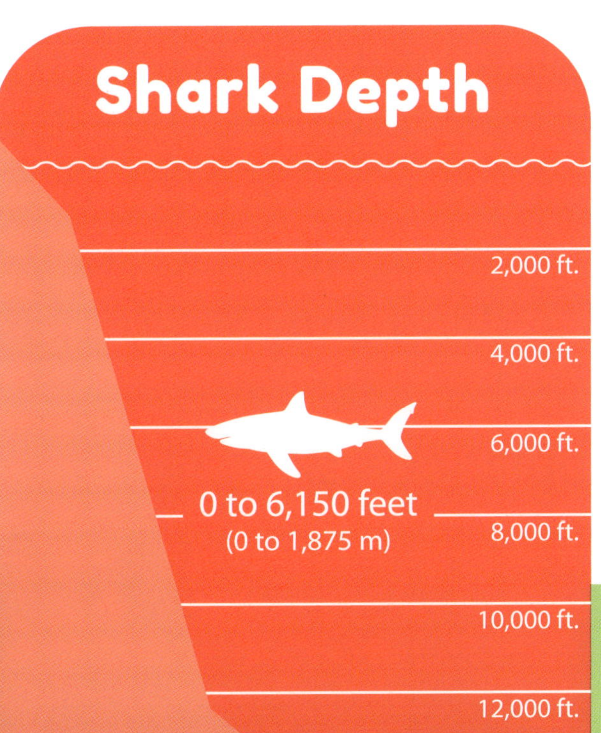

GREENLAND SHARK

(*Somniosus microcephalus*)

Appearance

Greenland sharks are large, slow-moving sharks. They can be black, brown, gray, or a mix of colors. They have 48 to 52 teeth on the upper jaw. There are 50 to 52 teeth on the lower jaw.

Length: Usually 7.9 to 14 feet (2.4 to 4.3 m)

Weight: 0.8 to 1.1 tons (0.7 to 1 metric ton)

Behavior

Greenland sharks are the longest-living vertebrate. Scientists think they can live 272 years or longer. They catch prey by sneaking up on it. They also feed on dead animals such as smaller sharks, seals, and polar bears.

A diver swims alongside a Greenland shark in Canada's Saint Lawrence River.

Range

Greenland sharks live in the cold waters of the Arctic and north Atlantic Oceans. They are also found in the North Sea and near the eastern coast of the United States. They mostly stay in deep water but can come to the surface.

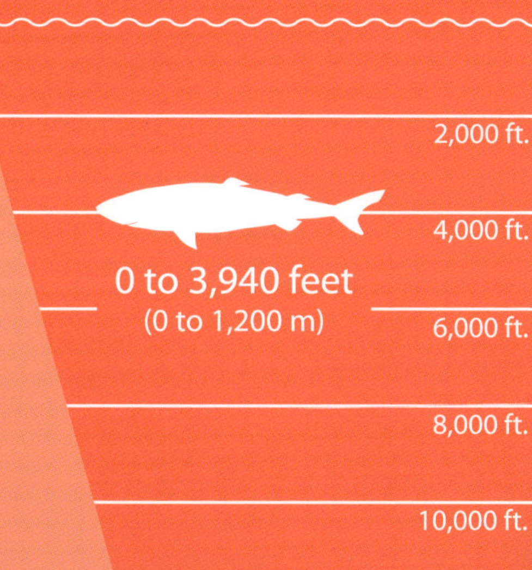

GULPER SHARK

(*Centrophorus granulosus*)

Appearance

Gulper sharks are dark gray or grayish brown. Their undersides are lighter. The gulper shark has a short, thick snout. Its eyes are big and green. Gulper sharks can live for more than 30 years.

Behavior

The gulper shark feeds on fish, squid, and crustaceans. It migrates in small schools. It stays on or near the ocean floor. A mother gulper shark carries her baby for two years before it is born. A newborn gulper is about as long as a ruler.

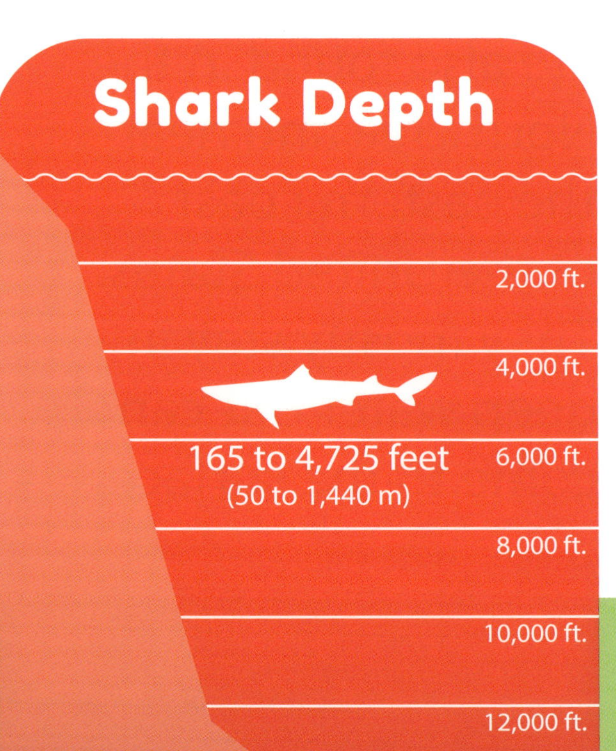

A diver poses with a gulper shark near the Bahamas.

Range

Gulper sharks are found in the Atlantic and Indian Oceans. They also live in the western and central Pacific Ocean. Because they live in deep water, they are rarely seen by humans.

Length: 3.4 to 3.6 feet (1 to 1.1 m)

Weight: Weight not documented

(*Heterodontus francisci*)

Appearance

The horn shark has a short head. It has ridges over its eyes. Horn sharks are brown with brown or black spots. Their undersides are yellow. These colors help them blend in with the ocean floor. They have spines on each dorsal fin.

Behavior

Horn sharks rest among rocks during the day. At night they come out to hunt for food. Horn sharks eat small fish and invertebrates. They wait for their prey to swim by. Then they attack and eat it. Sometimes horn sharks don't swim. They crawl instead.

Shark Depth

Usually 6.6 to 36 feet
(2 to 11 m)

2,000 ft.
4,000 ft.
6,000 ft.
8,000 ft.
10,000 ft.
12,000 ft.

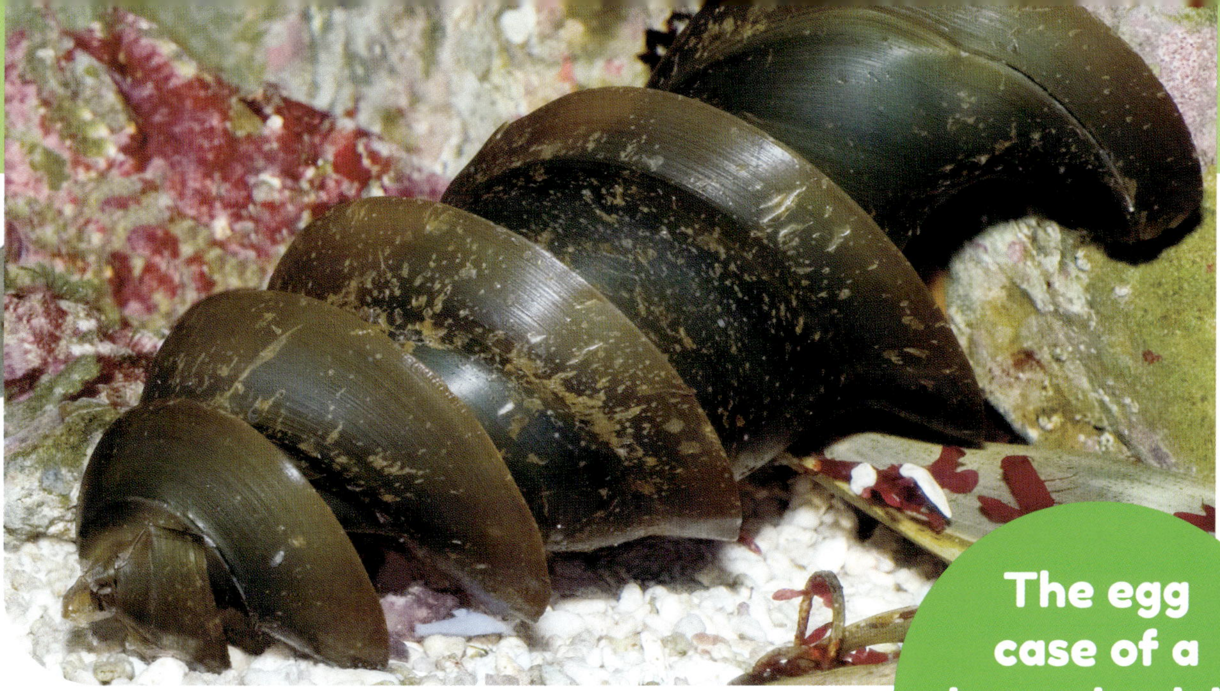

The egg case of a horn shark is shaped like a corkscrew.

They use their side fins to crawl along rocks.

Range

The horn shark is found in the eastern Pacific Ocean. It stays near the ocean floor in shallow areas. It hides out in rocky areas, kelp beds, and caves.

Length: Around 3.3 feet (1 m)

Weight: Usually 22 pounds (10 kg)

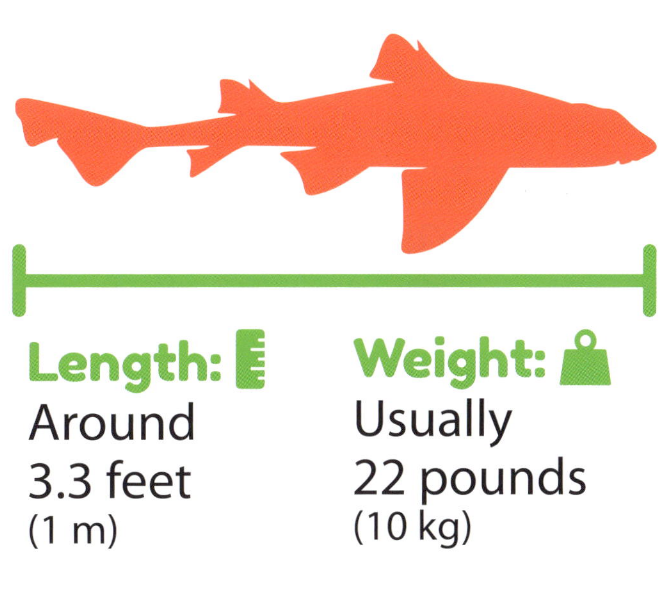

LEMON SHARK

(*Negaprion brevirostris*)

Appearance

The lemon shark is big and plump. Its snout is short. It has a flat head. The lemon shark is named for its yellowish-brown color. This helps it blend in with the sandy areas where it hunts for food.

Fish called suckerfish sometimes attach themselves to sharks. Suckerfish protect sharks from pests.

Behavior

Lemon sharks are active at night. A part of their eyes called the retina lets them see small details and colors underwater. They swim near docks, creeks,

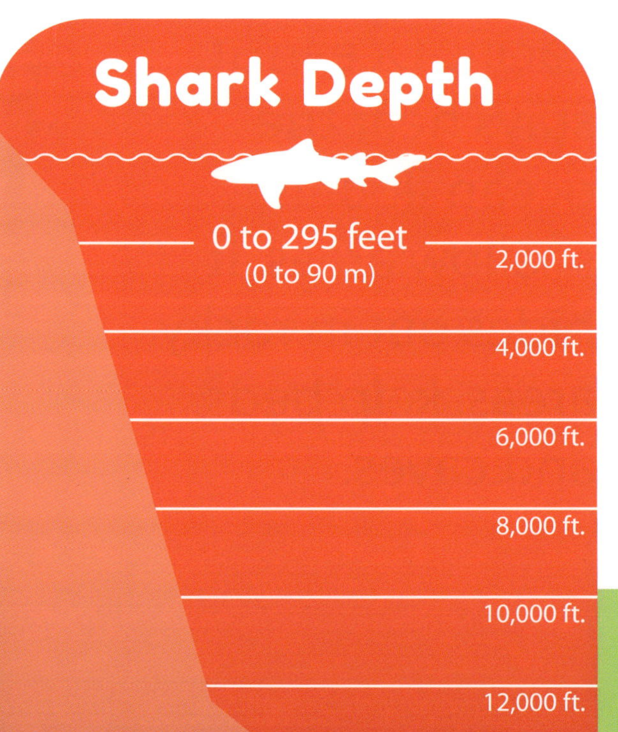

and bays. Sometimes they move in groups of about 20 while feeding. They eat fish, small sharks, and birds.

Range

Lemon sharks are found in the western Atlantic Ocean. They are also seen in the eastern north Atlantic Ocean and the eastern Pacific Ocean. They live in shallow coastal waters.

Length: 8.2 to 9.8 feet (2.5 to 3 m)

Weight: 550 pounds (250 kg)

LEOPARD SHARK

(*Triakis semifasciata*)

Leopard sharks are named for their leopard-like markings.

Appearance

Leopard sharks have skin patterns like a leopard's. Stripes and spots in different colors cover a leopard shark's back and sides. Its back is light gray or bronze. Its underside is lighter.

Behavior

Leopard sharks travel in groups called schools.

Length: Usually 3.9 to 4.9 feet (1.2 to 1.5 m)

Weight: Usually 40 pounds (18 kg)

Male sharks travel with other males. The same is true for females. Schools usually have sharks of similar sizes. Leopard sharks feed on invertebrates. They can travel several miles to find food. They are not bothered by other sharks who feed in the same place.

Range

Leopard sharks live in the eastern Pacific Ocean. They can be found from Oregon to California. They usually stay where the water is warm and shallow.

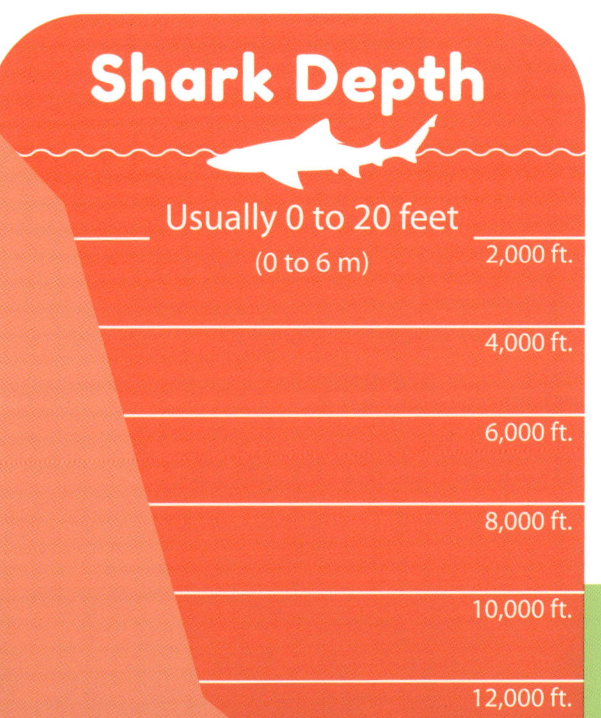

MEGAMOUTH SHARK

(*Megachasma pelagios*)

Appearance

The megamouth shark is named for its huge mouth. The upper part of its tail fin is much longer than the lower part. Its dorsal side is blackish brown. Its belly is white. There is a white band along the top of the snout. The megamouth's skin is loose and wrinkly.

Megamouths swim in deeper water during the day and shallower water at night.

Behavior

Megamouths swim slowly through areas of krill, or tiny crustaceans.

Shark Depth

2,000 ft.
4,000 ft.
15 to 4,920 feet
(5 to 1,500 m)
6,000 ft.
8,000 ft.
10,000 ft.
12,000 ft.

They keep their mouths open as they swim. This lets them suck in the krill. When they close their mouths, they swallow the krill. The extra water goes out through their gills.

Range

Megamouths can live both near the surface and in the deep sea. They spend most of their lives far from shore. This means they are rarely seen.

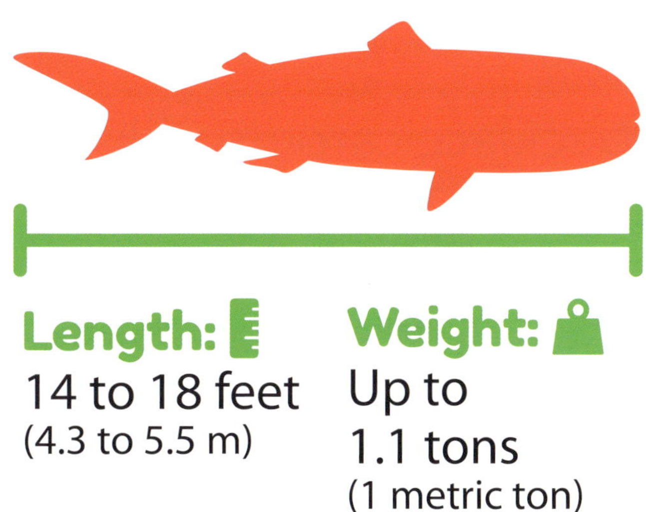

Length:
14 to 18 feet
(4.3 to 5.5 m)

Weight:
Up to
1.1 tons
(1 metric ton)

NECKLACE CARPETSHARK

(Parascyllium variolatum)

Appearance

Carpetsharks get their name from the patterns on their skin. These patterns are like those on a carpet. The necklace carpetshark has a thick black collar with white dots behind its head. This pattern looks kind of like a necklace. The necklace carpetshark is long and thin. It can be gray or brown. It has short barbels on its snout.

Necklace carpetsharks swim on the ocean floor.

Behavior

Necklace carpetsharks are shy. They are rarely seen during the day. They hunt at night. Scientists think

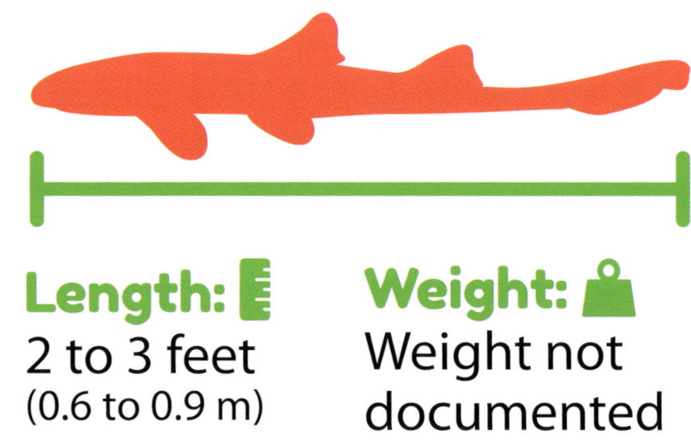

they probably eat invertebrates. Necklace carpetsharks are harmless to humans.

Range

Necklace carpetsharks are found near southern Australia. They swim on the ocean floor. They can be found near sandy bottoms and rocky reefs.

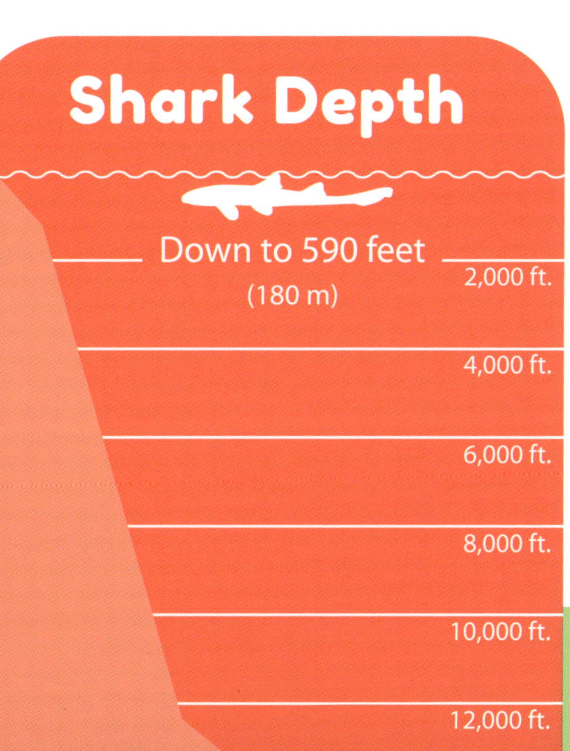

NURSE SHARK

(Ginglymostoma cirratum)

Nurse sharks often sleep together in caves.

Appearance

Nurse sharks are shades of gray, yellow, and brown. They have barbels on their snouts. Young nurse sharks have dark patches.

Behavior

Nurse sharks eat small fish and invertebrates.

Length: 3.6 to 9.8 feet (1.1 to 3 m)

Weight: 155 to 252 pounds (70.5 to 114.5 kg)

They hunt at night and rest during the day. Sometimes they rest in groups of up to 40 sharks. They lean against each other or pile up. Scientists are not sure why they do this. Nurse sharks are known for being quiet and peaceful.

Range

Nurse sharks are found in the western Atlantic Ocean, the Gulf of Mexico, and the Caribbean Sea. They can also be found in the eastern Atlantic and Pacific Oceans. These sharks sometimes swim near the coast of West Africa too.

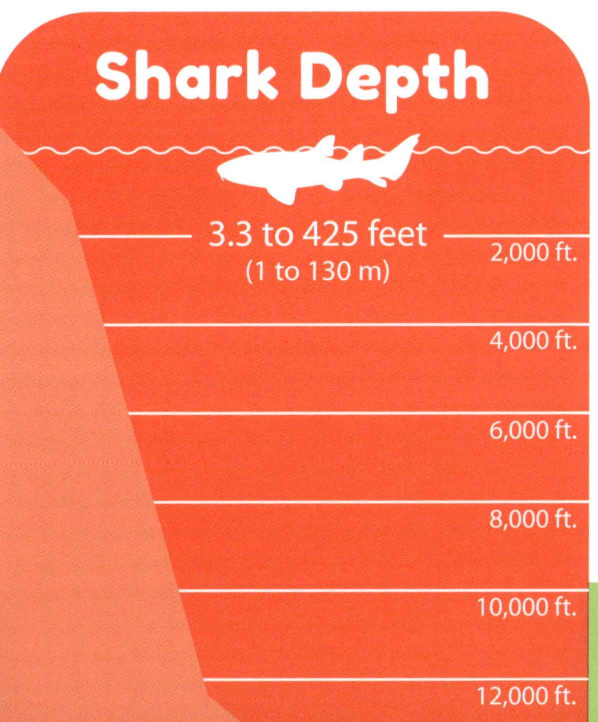

OCEANIC WHITETIP SHARK

(*Carcharhinus longimanus*)

Oceanic whitetip sharks have rounded, white-tipped fins.

Appearance

Oceanic whitetip sharks have big, thick bodies. Their name comes from the white marks on the tips of their fins. Their fins are rounded at the ends. Their bodies can be gray, bronze,

Shark Depth

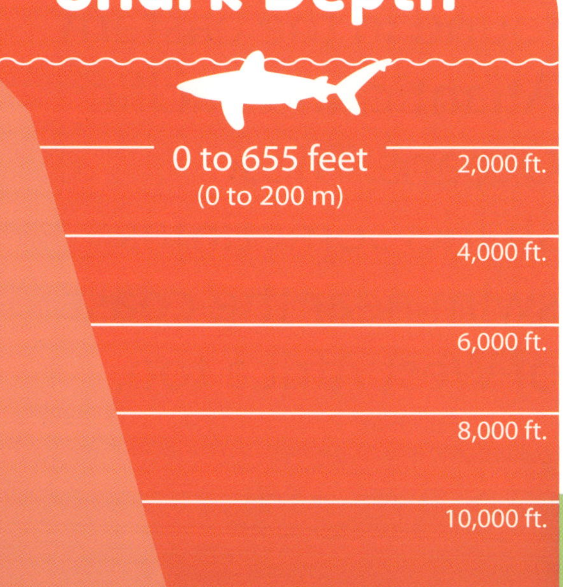

or brown. Their undersides are white or yellow. Oceanic whitetip sharks can live for 25 years.

Behavior

Oceanic whitetip sharks have big, paddle-like fins. These let them glide through the water. These sharks swim long distances in search of food. They sometimes follow fishing ships in hopes of finding a meal. They feed on fish and squid. They also eat seabirds and other sharks.

Range

Oceanic whitetip sharks are found around the world. They prefer tropical waters. They stay away from the shore.

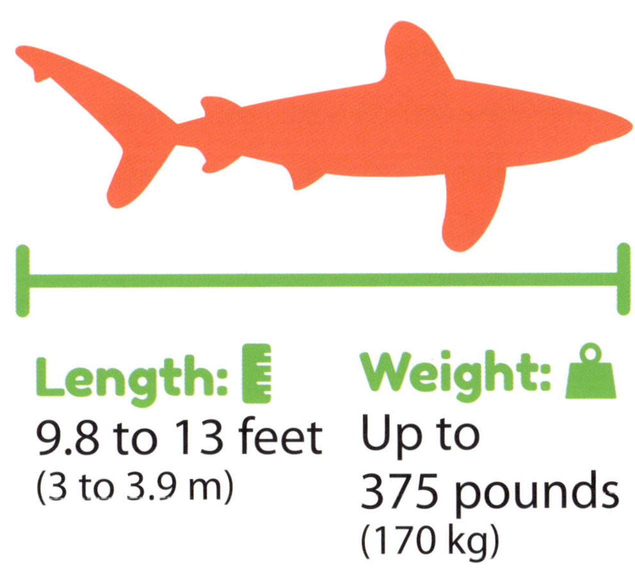

ORNATE WOBBEGONG

(*Orectolobus ornatus*)

Ornate wobbegongs blend into their environments.

Appearance

The ornate wobbegong shark has a wide, flat body. A fringe of barbels sticks out from the front of its face. Its body is usually golden with brown spots. Sometimes it has a green tinge. This coloring camouflages it well on the ocean floor.

Shark Depth

0 to 330 feet
(0 to 100 m)

2,000 ft.
4,000 ft.
6,000 ft.
8,000 ft.
10,000 ft.
12,000 ft.

Behavior

Ornate wobbegongs hunt for food at night. They feed on fish, crustaceans, sharks, and rays. They stay still until prey comes near. Then they grab it with their jaws. When surprised by a human, an ornate wobbegong may bite.

Length: Up to 3.9 feet (1.2 m)

Weight: Weight not documented

Range

These sharks are found in the western Pacific Ocean. They can be found all the way around the coast of Australia. They live on rocky bottoms and near coral reefs.

PACIFIC ANGELSHARK

(*Squatina californica*)

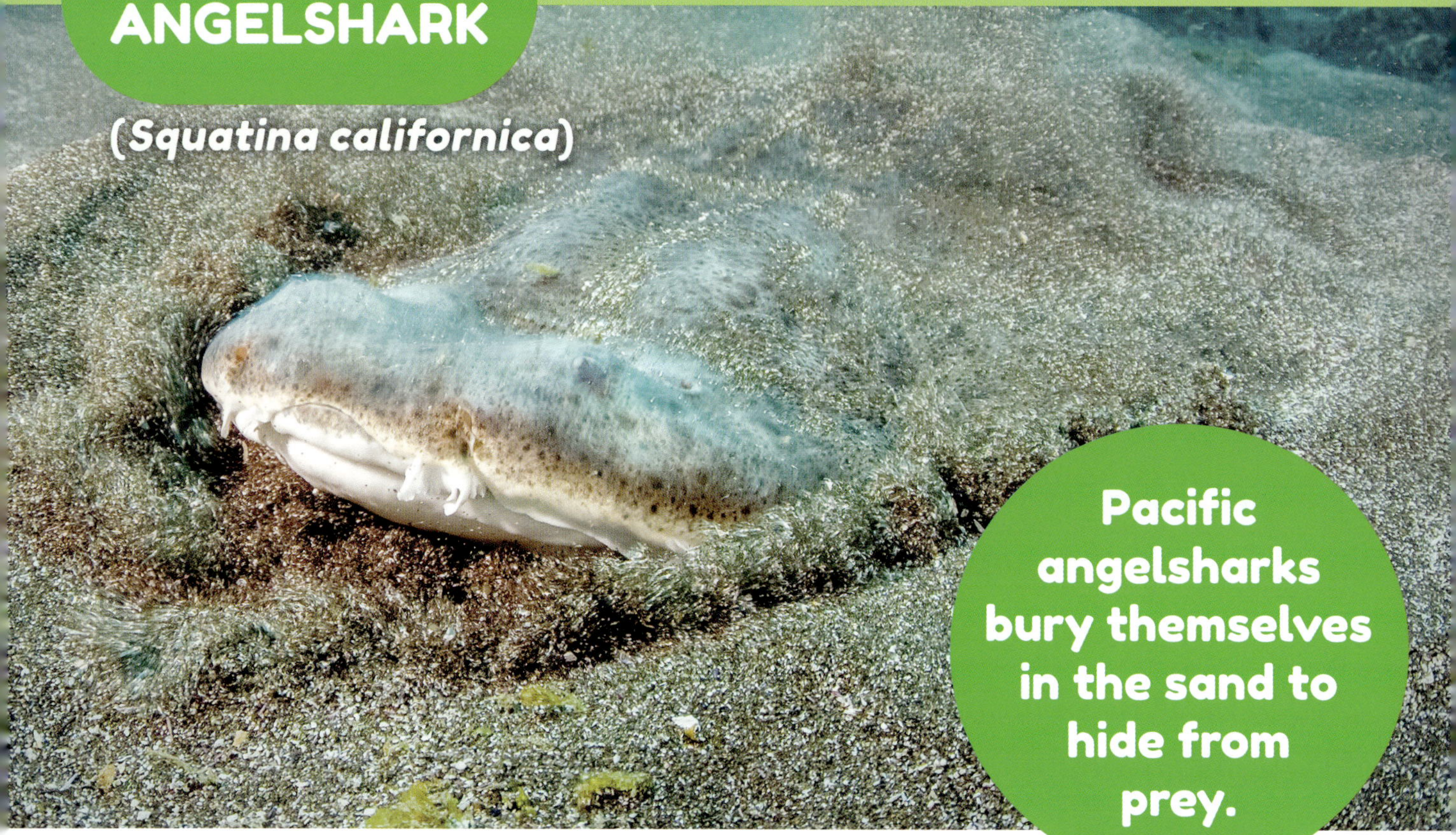

Pacific angelsharks bury themselves in the sand to hide from prey.

Appearance

The Pacific angelshark has a flat body. It looks like a ray or a skate. Gill slits lie on the sides of its head. It has a large mouth.

Length:
3.9 to
4.9 feet
(1.2 to 1.5 m)

Weight:
Up to
60 pounds
(27 kg)

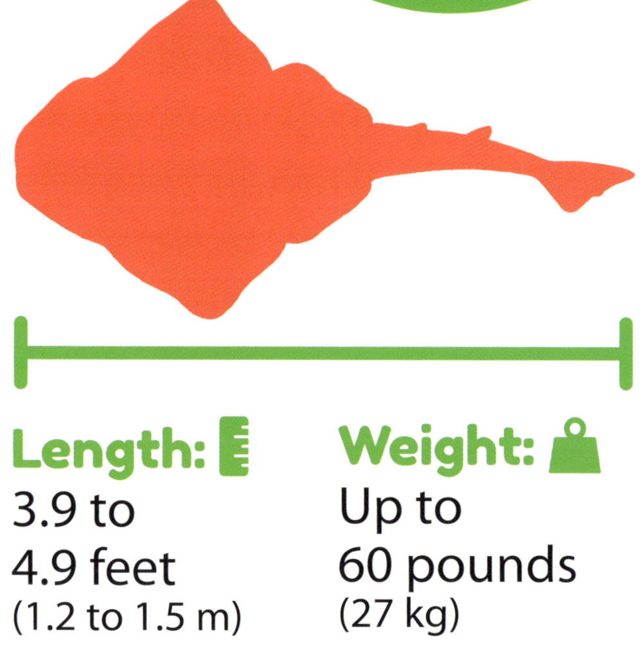

Behavior

The Pacific angelshark buries itself under the sand. When a fish swims by, the shark strikes. It sucks the fish into its big mouth. Then it swallows the fish whole. Many sharks must swim to breathe. But a Pacific angelshark can stay buried for weeks. It has muscles that pump water over its gills. This lets the shark breathe without swimming.

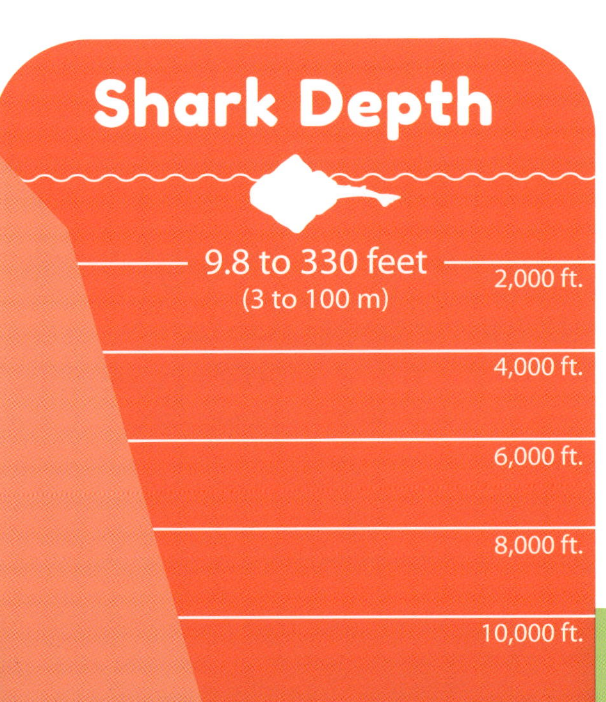

Range

This shark lives in shallow waters. It stays near the shoreline. It lives in the eastern Pacific Ocean.

PORBEAGLE SHARK

(*Lamna nasus*)

Appearance

Porbeagle sharks have heavy bodies and big gill slits. They have crescent-shaped tails. Their snouts are long and cone shaped. Their bodies are shaped like a porpoise's. They are good hunters, like beagles. These features led to the name *porbeagle*.

Behavior

Porbeagles are found both alone and in groups. They are active and playful. They ram floating objects with their snouts. They chase each other.

Length:
5.6 to 12 feet
(1.7 to 3.7 m)

Weight:
Usually
300 pounds
(135 kg)

Porbeagle shark teeth are smooth.

They sometimes leap all the way out of the water when hunting. Porbeagles feed on fish and shellfish.

Range

Porbeagle sharks are found in cold water in the north Atlantic Ocean. They have also been seen off the coast of Argentina. They mostly stay in deep waters.

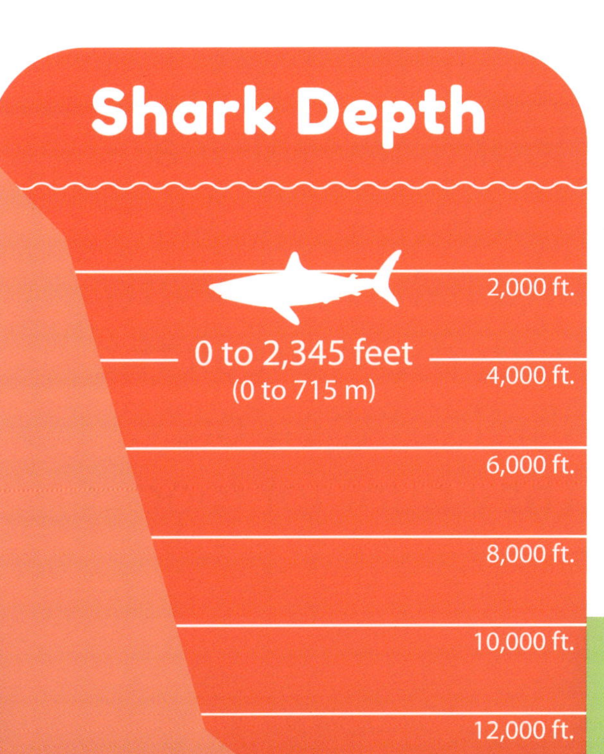

PORT JACKSON SHARK

(*Heterodontus portusjacksoni*)

Appearance

The Port Jackson shark has a big bump on its head. Its dorsal side is gray. The shark has black patches over its eyes and along its sides. The front teeth are small and sharp. The back teeth are wide and flat.

Behavior

Port Jackson sharks live on the ocean floor. They eat sea urchins, mollusks, and fish. Their teeth help them break the shells of their prey. They hunt for food

Length: Usually 3 feet (0.9 m)

Weight: 13 to 31 pounds (6 to 14 kg)

Port Jackson sharks lay spiral-shaped egg cases.

at night. During the day, they stay in caves or under rocks for safety. They can also be found near seagrasses.

Range

Port Jackson sharks are found in southern Australian waters. They live near rocky areas or on the ocean floor. They also like muddy or sandy areas with seagrasses.

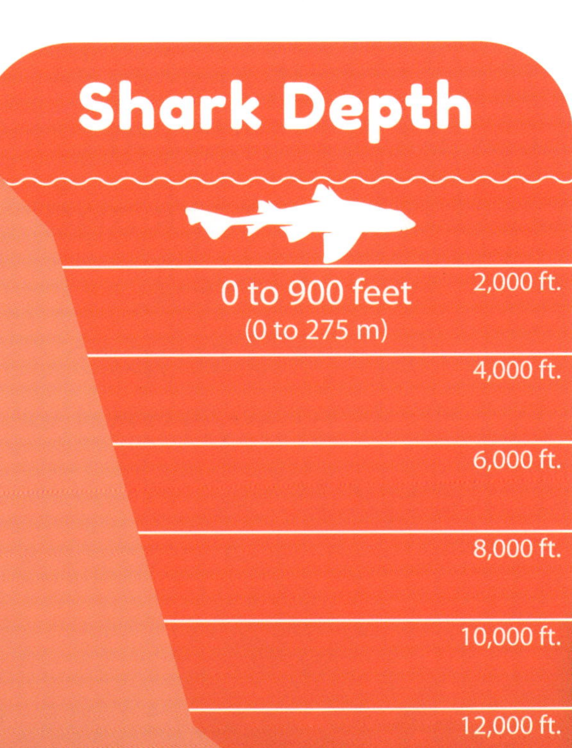

PUFFADDER SHYSHARK

(Haploblepharus edwardsii)

Puffadder shysharks curl up to defend themselves.

Appearance

The puffadder shyshark is skinny. It is usually shorter than a tennis racket. It has a round snout and oval eyes with eyelids. Its sand-brown back and sides are covered with dark-red stripes and dark-brown and white spots.

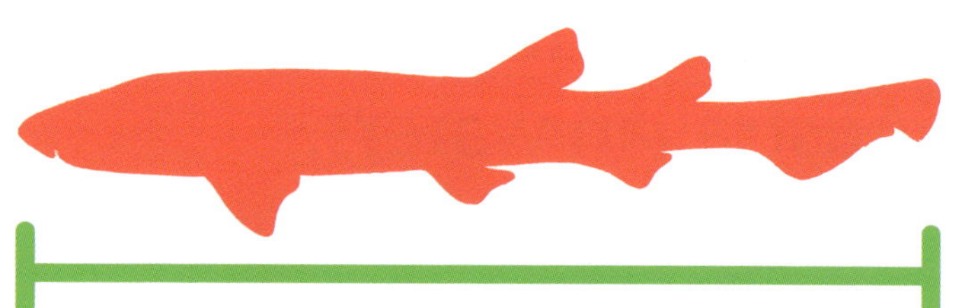

Length: Up to 2 feet (0.6 m)

Weight: Weight not documented

Behavior

Puffadder shysharks rest on the ocean floor. They curl up with their tail fins on top of their heads. This protects their eyes. It also makes it hard for predators such as seals to swallow them whole. Puffadder shysharks eat small fish, crabs, shrimp, and squid.

Range

Puffadder shysharks are found along the southern coast of Africa. They swim both near the coast and out in the open sea. They like sandy and rocky bottom areas.

Shark Depth

0 to 425 feet
(0 to 130 m)

2,000 ft.
4,000 ft.
6,000 ft.
8,000 ft.
10,000 ft.
12,000 ft.

SALMON SHARK

(*Lamna ditropis*)

Appearance

The salmon shark has a dark-gray back and white belly. It has a ridge on the lower part of its wide tail. It has big teeth and long gill slits.

Behavior

Salmon sharks are strong swimmers. They are called salmon sharks because they feed on Pacific salmon. They also eat squid and other fish. They migrate alone or in groups. Salmon sharks can keep their body temperatures warmer than the cold water around them.

Length: Usually 5.9 feet (1.8 m)

Weight: Up to 485 pounds (220 kg)

Salmon sharks are sometimes mistaken for great white or porbeagle sharks.

Range

Salmon sharks are found in the northern and western Pacific Ocean. They also live in the Bering Sea and the Sea of Japan. They swim both near the coast and out in the open sea.

Shark Depth

Usually 0 to 500 feet (0 to 152 m)

2,000 ft.
4,000 ft.
6,000 ft.
8,000 ft.
10,000 ft.
12,000 ft.

SAND TIGER SHARK

(Carcharias taurus)

Sand tiger sharks are sometimes called raggedtooth or gray nurse sharks.

Appearance

The sand tiger shark has a short, pointed snout. Its eyes are small. Its back is pale brown or gray. Its underside is lighter. People can see this shark's many sharp teeth even when its mouth is closed.

Length: Usually 4 to 9 feet (1.2 to 2.7 m)

Weight: Usually 210 to 245 pounds (95 to 110 kg)

Behavior

The sand tiger shark swims slowly with its mouth open. Water passing over its gills helps it to breathe. Sometimes it will gulp air at the water's surface. The air goes into its stomach. This helps the shark float. The shark feeds on fish, small sharks, rays, and shellfish.

Range

Sand tiger sharks are found in the western and eastern Atlantic Ocean. They are also found in the western Indian and Pacific Oceans. These sharks also swim in the western Mediterranean Sea. Sand tiger sharks like warm ocean regions.

Shark Depth

6.6 to 627 feet
(2 to 191 m)

2,000 ft.
4,000 ft.
6,000 ft.
8,000 ft.
10,000 ft.
12,000 ft.

SANDBAR SHARK

(*Carcharhinus plumbeus*)

Appearance

The sandbar shark is brownish gray. It has a thick body, a short snout, and a wide mouth. Its teeth are serrated.

Behavior

The sandbar shark stays on the sandy ocean floor in coastal areas. It is also found in areas where rivers or bays meet the sea. It feeds on fish, eels, skates, rays, and shellfish. It is more active at night than during the day. The sandbar shark migrates north during warmer

Length: 7.9 to 9.8 feet (2.4 to 3 m)

Weight: 110 to 150 pounds (50 to 70 kg)

Sandbar sharks give birth to live young.

months and south during colder months. Some sandbar sharks move to a new location because they are carried by ocean currents.

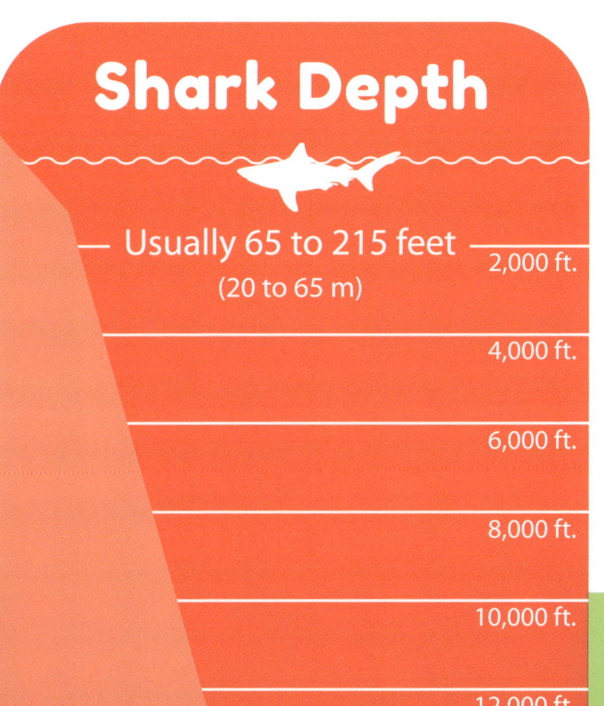

Range

The sandbar shark lives near the coast and in the open seas. It prefers warm water. This shark is found around the world.

SCALLOPED HAMMERHEAD SHARK

(*Sphyrna lewini*)

Appearance

The scalloped hammerhead shark's head is shaped like a double-headed hammer. The shark's eyes are on the ends of the hammer shape. The front part of the shark's head has bumps, or scallops. This shark has a small mouth.

Behavior

This shark stays close to the shore during the day. At night it hunts in the open ocean. It feeds on fish, shellfish, and smaller sharks. It has special sensors on

Length: 7.2 to 11 feet (2.2 to 3.5 m)

Weight: Up to 335 pounds (152 kg)

its head. These sensors can feel when other sea life is near. They help the shark find prey buried in the sand.

The scalloped hammerhead shark's head shape differs from other hammerhead sharks.

Range

These sharks prefer warm waters. They swim along coasts. They are found in the Red Sea, the Atlantic and Pacific Oceans, and the Caribbean Sea.

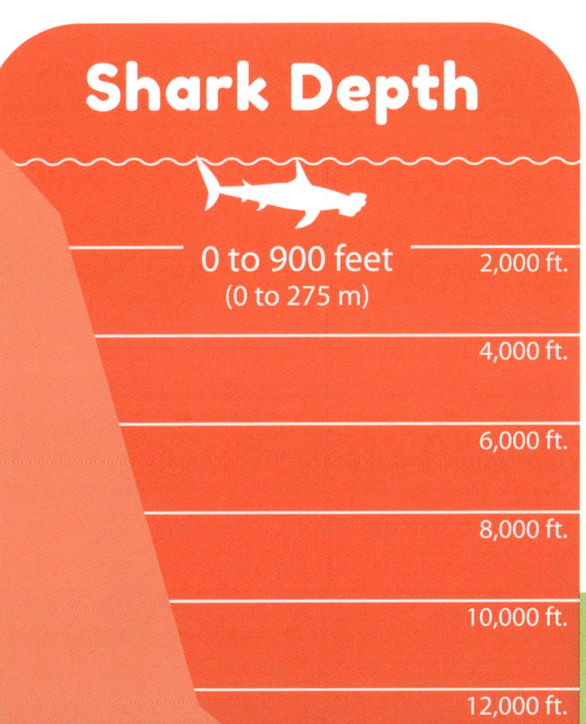

SCHOOL SHARK

(*Galeorhinus galeus*)

School sharks are also called tope sharks or soupfin sharks.

Appearance

The school shark is a small, thin shark. It has a long snout. The top part of its tail fin is much longer than the lower part. The shark's back is dark bluish gray. Its underside is white.

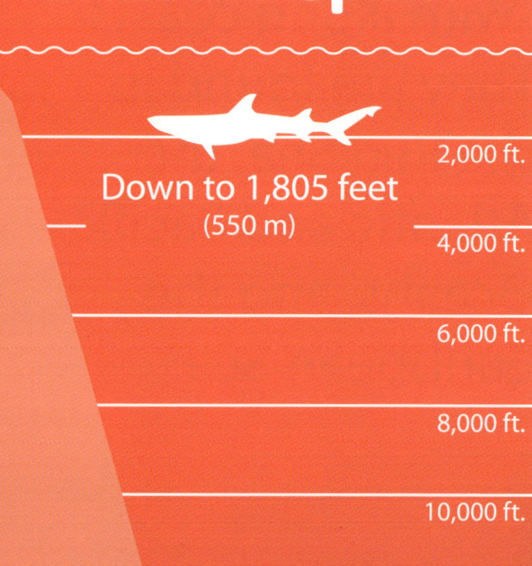

Large school sharks can grow up to 6.4 feet (2 m) long.

Behavior

School sharks can live for 55 years. They travel together in groups called schools. Sharks in a school all are about the same size. A school is either all male or all female. School sharks feed on fish, squid, and octopuses.

Range

School sharks are found in oceans around the world. They swim in both cold and warm areas. They can be found near the shore or offshore.

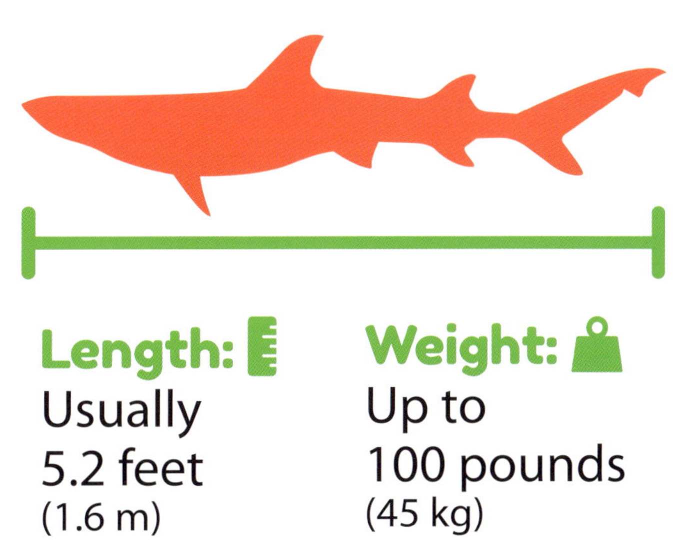

Length: Usually 5.2 feet (1.6 m)

Weight: Up to 100 pounds (45 kg)

SEVENGILL SHARK

(*Notorynchus cepedianus*)

Sevengill sharks have more gill slits than most sharks.

Appearance

Most sharks have five gill slits on each side of the body. The sevengill shark has seven. It has a thick body and a wide, blunt snout. The shark is silvery gray or brown. Sometimes it has spots. Its belly is white.

Length: Usually 4.9 feet (1.5 m)

Weight: Up to 236 pounds (107 kg)

Behavior

Sevengill sharks stay in shallow water. They prefer rocky or sandy ocean floors. Sevengills feed on almost anything. They eat rays, dolphins, seals, and fish, including other sharks. A sevengill shark digests its food very slowly. It can go weeks between feedings.

Range

Sevengill sharks are found in coastal regions around the world. They are also found in the open sea. They live in the Pacific and south Atlantic Oceans.

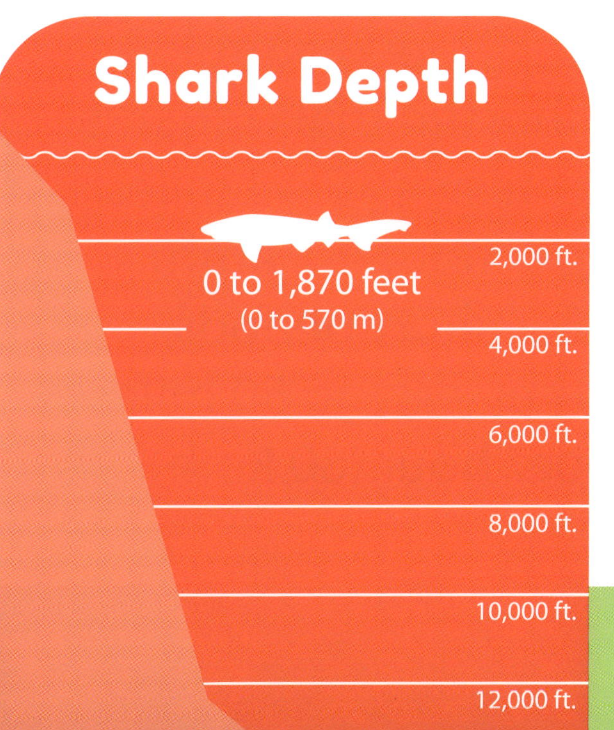

SHORTFIN MAKO SHARK

(Isurus oxyrinchus)

Appearance

Shortfin mako sharks have deep purple or blue backs. Their undersides are white. They have big eyes and five gill slits on each side of the body.

Behavior

Most sharks move at a speed of about 5 miles per hour (8 kmh). But shortfin mako sharks can swim 21.5 miles per hour (35 kmh). For short periods, they can go 50 miles per hour (80 kmh)!

Length: Usually 6.6 to 9.5 feet (2 to 2.9 m)

Weight: 130 to 330 pounds (60 to 150 kg)

Shortfin mako sharks are fast swimmers.

They can travel more than 1,300 miles (2,090 km) in a month. That is about halfway across the United States. Shortfin makos feed on tuna, squid, dolphins, and sea turtles.

Range

Shortfin mako sharks are found around the world. They live in the Pacific, Indian, and Atlantic Oceans. They also live in the Red Sea and the Mediterranean Sea.

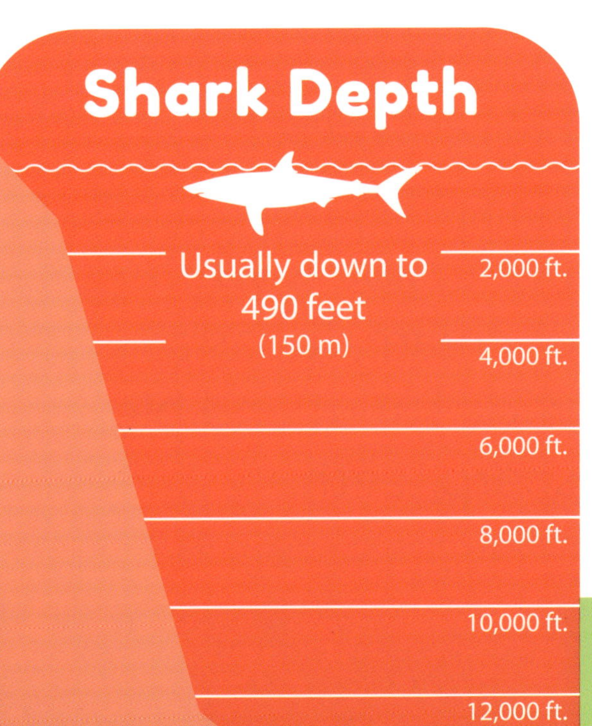

SICKLEFIN LEMON SHARK

(*Negaprion acutidens*)

Appearance

The sicklefin lemon shark has a big, thick body. It is twice as long as a twin-size bed. Its back is yellowish brown. Its underside is white or cream. It has a wide snout and big, sharp teeth.

Length: Up to 12 feet (3.8 m)

Weight: Up to 400 pounds (180 kg)

Sicklefin lemon sharks have curved fins.

Behavior

Sicklefin lemon sharks are shy and quiet. They will attack only if they are poked or speared. If this happens, they can be dangerous to humans. Sicklefin lemon sharks feed on smaller sharks, rays, and other fish. They do not migrate to hunt for food. They stay in one area instead.

Range

Sicklefin lemon sharks live in the Indian and Pacific Oceans. They can be found from South Africa to Australia. They also swim in the Red Sea.

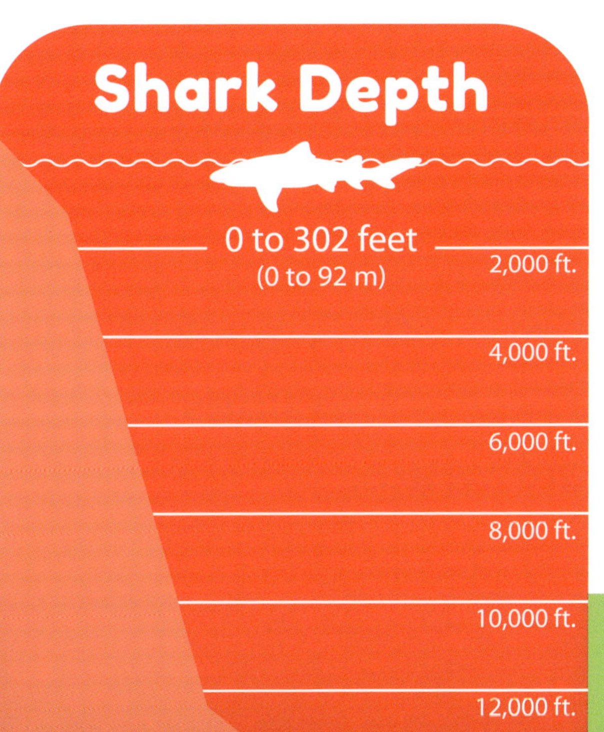

SILKY SHARK

(*Carcharhinus falciformis*)

There are many silky sharks in the open ocean.

Appearance

The silky shark has smooth, shiny skin. The upper part of its tail fin is long and pointed. The silky shark has a long snout. These sharks are dark gray with a bronze tint on their backs. Their undersides are white.

Length: Usually 8.2 feet (2.5 m)

Weight: 392 to 763 pounds (178 to 346 kg)

This shark can grow up to 11 feet (3.3 m) long. It lives for about 23 years.

Behavior

Silky sharks are one of the most commonly found sharks in the open water. They mostly stay away from the shore and the surface. They feed on tuna and other fish.

Range

Silky sharks live in tropical waters. They are found in the Atlantic, Pacific, and Indian Oceans. They mostly live in the open sea.

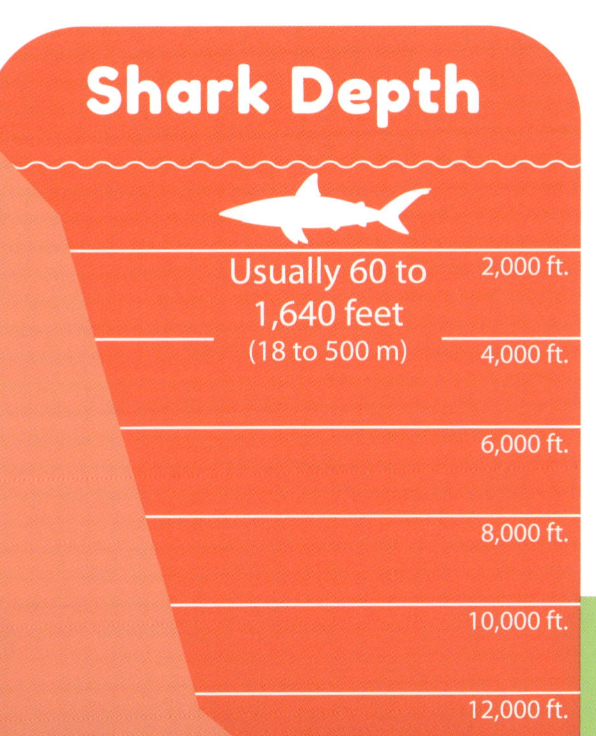

SILVERTIP SHARK

(*Carcharhinus albimarginatus*)

Appearance

Silvertip sharks have long snouts. Their eyes are big and round. They are dark gray or grayish brown. The underside is white. They are named for the shiny white tips and borders on their fins. They can grow to be as long as a ping-pong table. But they are usually shorter.

Silvertip sharks give birth to live young.

Behavior

Silvertip sharks are bold hunters. They feed on fish, rays, octopuses, squid, and small sharks. When they find food, they become lively

Length: Usually 6.6 to 8.2 feet (2 to 2.5 m)

Weight: Up to 358 pounds (162 kg)

and fierce. Sometimes they follow fishing boats to find a meal.

Range

Silvertip sharks are found near islands and coral reefs. They have been seen in the western Indian Ocean and the Red Sea. They are also found in the western and eastern Pacific Ocean.

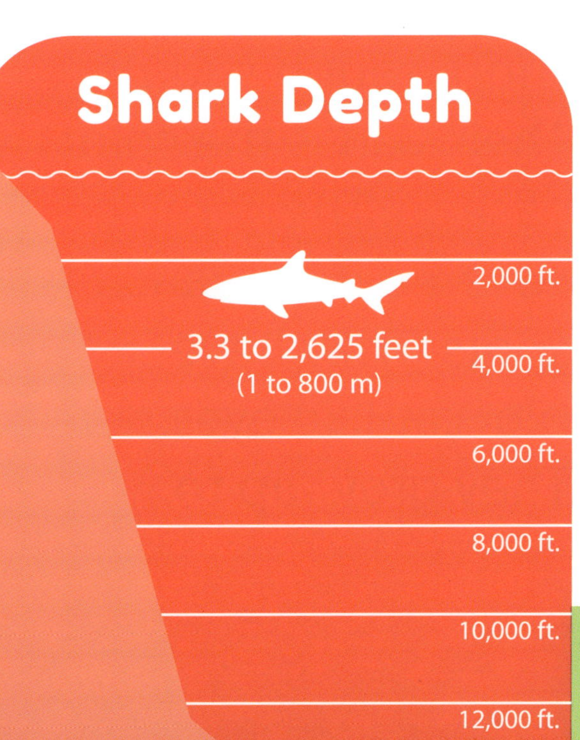

SMALL-SPOTTED CATSHARK

(*Scyliorhinus canicula*)

Small-spotted catsharks are sometimes called dogfish.

Appearance

Small-spotted catsharks are slim. They have short, round snouts. Their skin is the color of sand. They are covered with dark spots. They have big, cat-like eyes. They grow up to

Shark Depth

Usually 330 feet (100 m)

2,000 ft.
4,000 ft.
6,000 ft.
8,000 ft.
10,000 ft.
12,000 ft.

3.3 feet (1 m) long. But they are usually shorter.

Behavior

Small-spotted catsharks stay still during the day. They hunt prey at night. Small-spotted catsharks feed on mollusks and crustaceans. They also eat fish. They are harmless to humans.

Range

Small-spotted catsharks are found along the coasts of western Europe and northern Africa. They live on the ocean floor. They stay in shallow water.

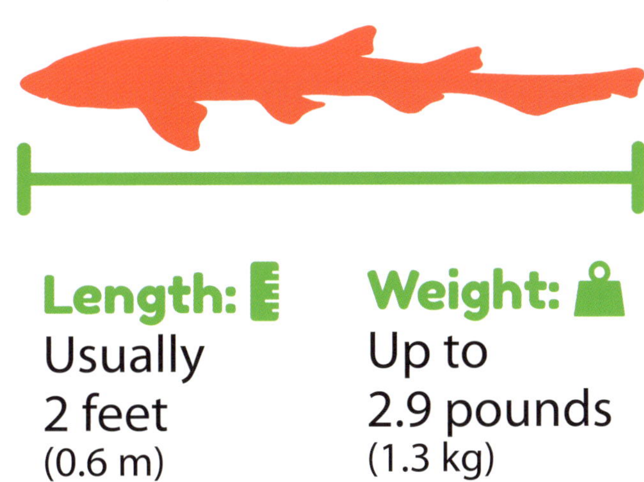

Length: Usually 2 feet (0.6 m)

Weight: Up to 2.9 pounds (1.3 kg)

SMALLEYE HAMMERHEAD SHARK

(*Sphyrna tudes*)

Smalleye hammerheads have smaller eyes than other hammerhead sharks.

Appearance

Smalleye hammerhead sharks can be bright gold, yellow, or orange. This shark has a wide, flat hammerhead. It is named for the tiny eyes on the sides of its hammerhead. Some people call this shark the golden hammerhead because of its color.

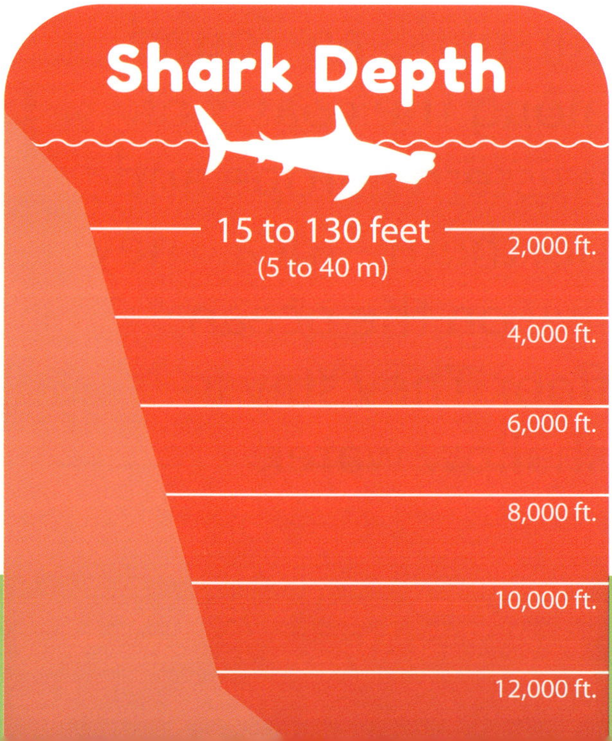

Shark Depth

15 to 130 feet (5 to 40 m)

2,000 ft.
4,000 ft.
6,000 ft.
8,000 ft.
10,000 ft.
12,000 ft.

This shark has a wide mouth. Its jaws are filled with long, thin teeth.

Length: Up to 4.9 feet (1.5 m)

Weight: 20 pounds (9 kg)

Behavior

Smalleye hammerheads feed on shrimp and catfish. Experts think their golden-orange color comes from the shrimp they eat. They have good vision for spotting prey.

Range

Smalleye hammerhead sharks are found mostly in muddy coastal waters. They live along the eastern coast of South America. They can be seen from Venezuela to Uruguay.

SPINNER SHARK

(*Carcharhinus brevipinna*)

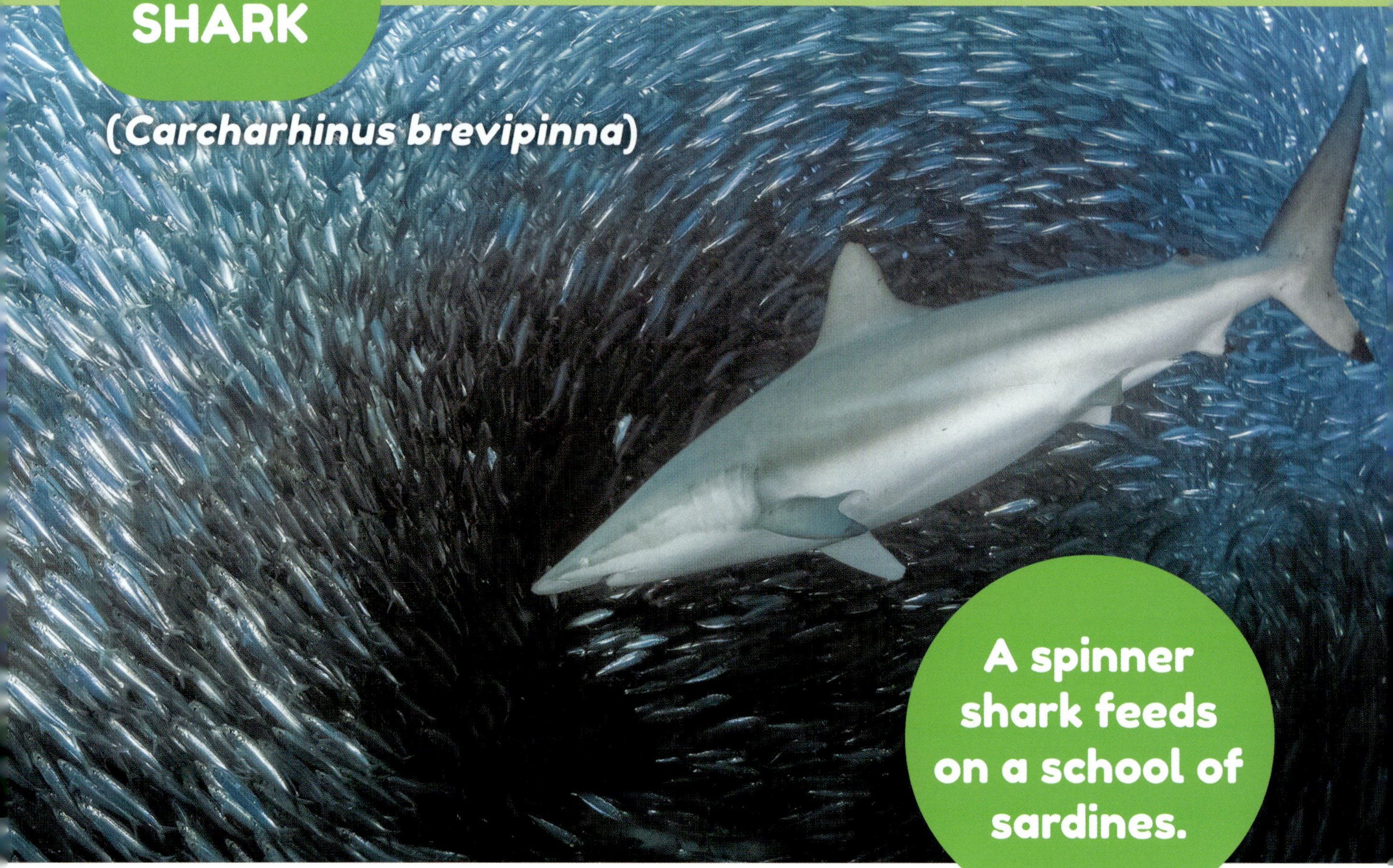

A spinner shark feeds on a school of sardines.

Appearance

The spinner shark is long and thin. It is gray or bronze on top. The belly and sides are white. It has a long, pointed snout.

Shark Depth

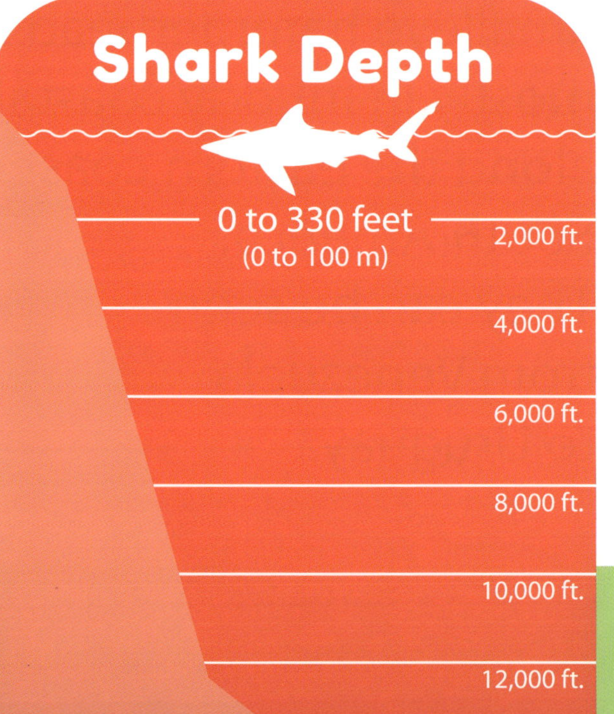

Behavior

Spinner sharks feed on fish, rays, and octopuses. They travel in schools. They have a special way of feeding. They swim at high speed through a school of fish. Then they do a spinning leap out of the water. This surprises their prey. While spinning, they open their mouths and snap their jaws.

Range

Spinner sharks are found in the warm parts of the Atlantic Ocean. They also live in the Indian and Pacific Oceans. They can be seen in the Mediterranean Sea. Spinner sharks also live in the Gulf of Mexico.

Length: Usually 6.4 feet (2 m)

Weight: Usually 123 pounds (56 kg)

SPINY DOGFISH SHARK

(*Squalus acanthias*)

Spiny dogfish sharks are not considered harmful to humans.

Appearance

The spiny dogfish shark has sharp spines on each of its two dorsal fins. The shark's back is gray or brown.

Length: Usually 2.3 to 3.3 feet (0.7 to 1 m)

Weight: 6.8 to 20 pounds (3.1 to 9.1 kg)

Its underside is light gray or white. Most spiny dogfish sharks live 25 to 30 years.

Behavior

Spiny dogfish sharks travel in schools like packs of dogs. This is where they get their name. Hundreds to thousands of sharks can be in a school. Spiny dogfish eat fish, small sharks, squid, and crabs.

Range

Spiny dogfish swim in the northern Pacific and northern Atlantic Oceans. They also live in the Mediterranean and Black Seas. They like areas that are not too hot or cold.

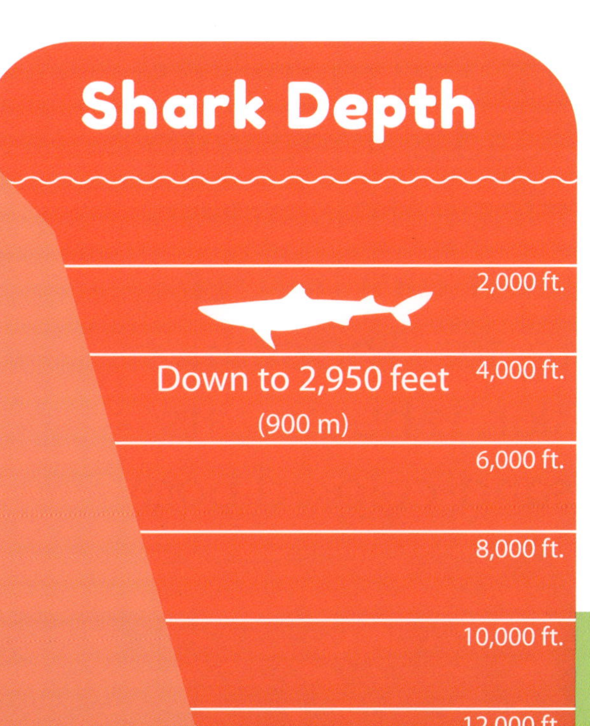

TASSELLED WOBBEGONG

(*Eucrossorhinus dasypogon*)

Tasselled wobbegongs are masters of camouflage.

Appearance

The tasselled wobbegong is flat and round. Its head is lined with a fringe. This makes the head harder to see. The shark's skin is bumpy. Its sand-colored body

Length: Up to 4.3 feet (1.3 m)

Weight: More than 154 pounds (70 kg)

has a pattern of dark lines and spots. This coloring helps camouflage the shark. It blends in with the reef around it.

Behavior

Tasselled wobbegongs feed on fish and invertebrates. They are active at night. When prey approaches, the shark opens its mouth and sucks in the prey.

Range

Tasselled wobbegongs swim in the western Pacific Ocean. They live near Australia, eastern Indonesia, and New Guinea. They stay in or near offshore reefs.

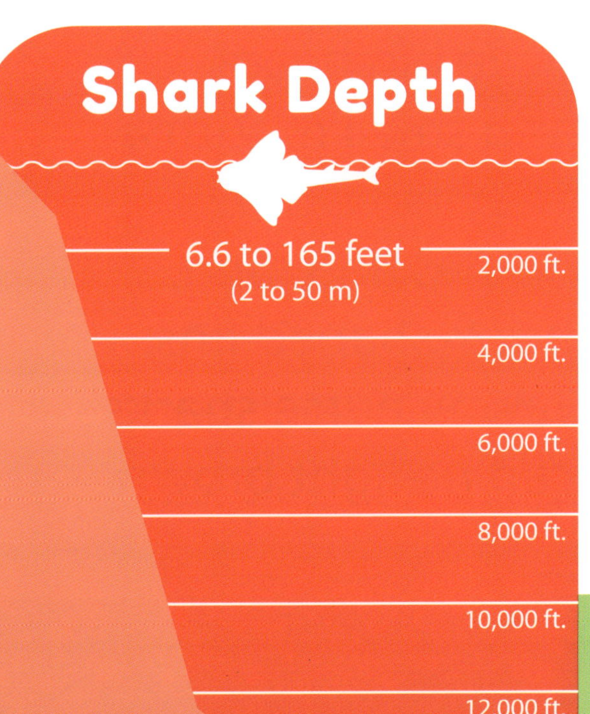

TAWNY NURSE SHARK

(*Nebrius ferrugineus*)

The tawny nurse shark is sometimes called the giant sleepy shark.

Appearance

Tawny nurse sharks have big heads and small mouths. They have thin bodies and long, hook-shaped fins. Tawny nurse sharks can be light brown

Length: Usually 8.2 feet (2.5 m)

Weight: 230 to 330 pounds (105 to 150 kg)

or dark brown. They can change color to match their habitats.

Behavior

Tawny nurse sharks are active at night. They usually stay near reefs. Sometimes these sharks will rest together in a pile. They feed on invertebrates. If prey is too big, the shark will spit it out and suck it back in. This tears the food into smaller pieces.

Range

Tawny nurse sharks are found in the Indian and Pacific Oceans. They live in warm, shallow waters. The sharks are mostly active at night.

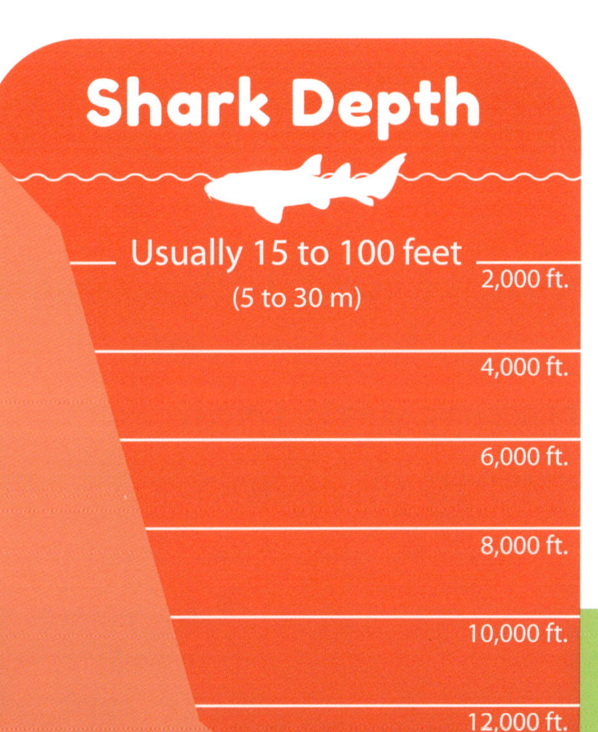

(*Galeocerdo cuvier*)

Young tiger shark

Appearance

Tiger sharks have gray backs and white bellies. They are named for the stripes on the sides of their young. These look like tiger stripes. As the sharks get older, these patterns fade.

Behavior

Tiger sharks feed on turtles, rays, smaller sharks, dolphins, and birds. They are slow swimmers. But they can use a burst of speed to catch prey. They crack the shells of turtles with their strong jaws and

Length: Usually 11 to 14 feet (3.3 to 4.3 m)

Weight: More than 850 to 1,400 pounds (385 to 635 kg)

Adult tiger shark

sharp teeth. Tiger sharks clean up the ocean floor by eating dead animals.

Range

Tiger sharks are found around the world. They swim in warm, tropical waters. They live in the oceans around North and South America, Africa, India, and Australia.

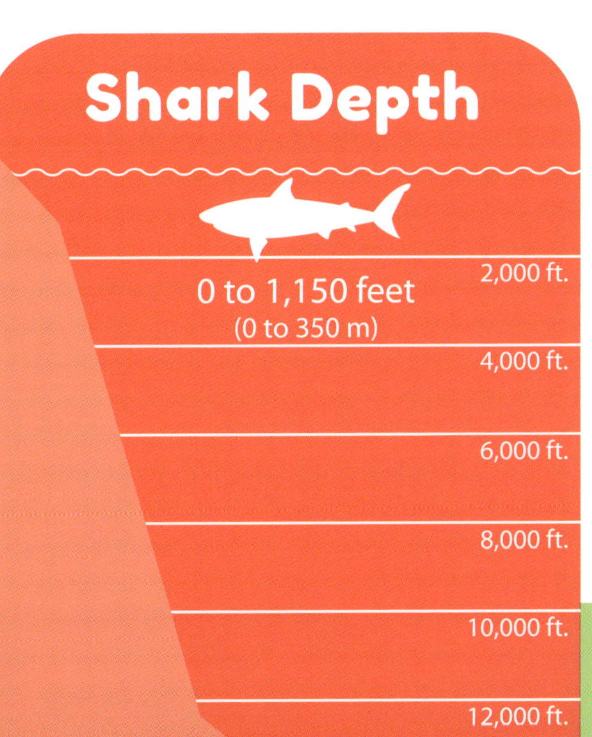

WHALE SHARK

(*Rhincodon typus*)

A whale shark can open its mouth and suck in prey like a giant vacuum cleaner.

Appearance

The whale shark is the biggest shark in the ocean. It has a wide, flat head. Its mouth is huge. Its skin is gray, blue, or green. The whale shark has a dorsal pattern

Length: Usually 23 to 33 feet (7 to 10 m)

Weight: Up to 34 tons (31 metric tons)

of yellow or white spots and stripes. Its underside is white or yellow. Whale sharks can grow up to 66 feet (20 m) long.

Behavior

Whale sharks are gentle and calm. They migrate long distances. They travel for as long as 37 months. They feed on plankton. To eat, whale sharks suck in water and swallow the small plankton living in it.

Range

Whale sharks are found in the open sea. They also live near the coast. They are found around the world wherever water is warm.

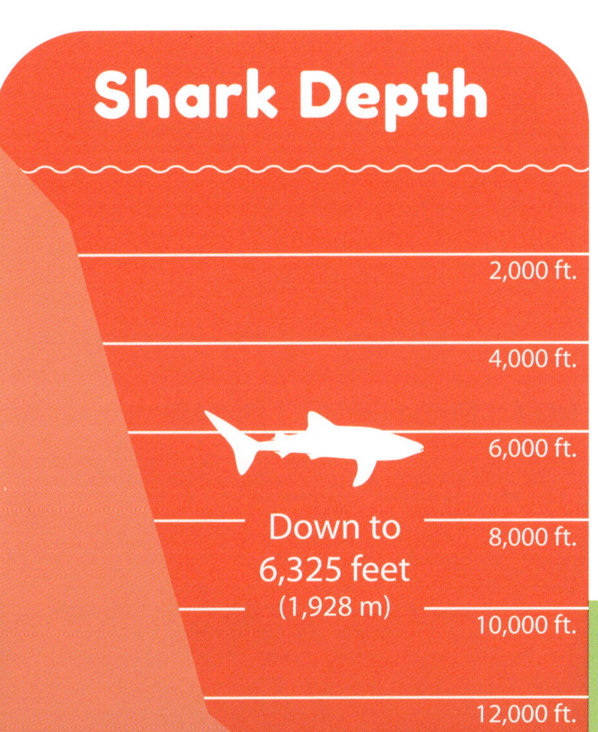

WHITESPOTTED BAMBOO SHARK

(Chiloscyllium plagiosum)

Whitespotted bamboo sharks lay eggs.

Appearance

The whitespotted bamboo shark is a small carpetshark. Like other carpetsharks, it has a carpet-like pattern on its body. It has dark-brown stripes.It also has white, blue, and black spots. It has a long, thin body. There are barbels near each nostril.

Shark Depth

0 to 165 feet
(0 to 50 m)

2,000 ft.
4,000 ft.
6,000 ft.
8,000 ft.
10,000 ft.
12,000 ft.

Behavior

The whitespotted bamboo shark glides along coral reefs. It also swims on the ocean floor. It eats small fish and invertebrates. It is active during the night. Whitespotted bamboo sharks are harmless to humans.

Range

Whitespotted bamboo sharks are found around the coast of Madagascar. This is an island off the east coast of Africa. They also swim in the waters between India and Indonesia.

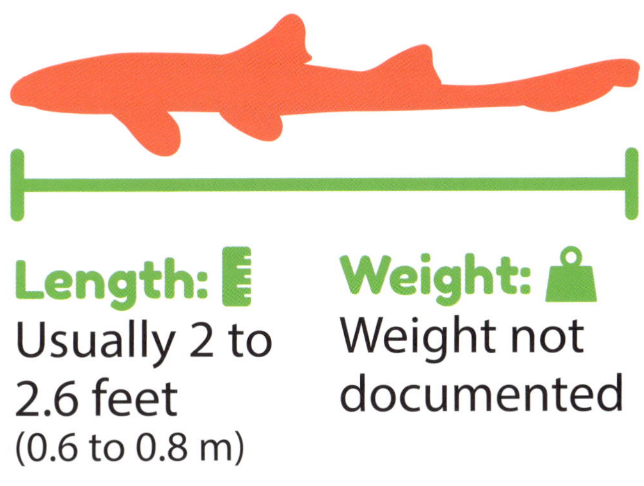

Length: Usually 2 to 2.6 feet (0.6 to 0.8 m)

Weight: Weight not documented

WHITETIP REEF SHARK

(Triaenodon obesus)

Whitetip reef sharks live in coral reefs and caves.

Appearance

The whitetip reef shark's dorsal side is gray or brown. The shark is named for the white tips of its dorsal and tail fins. Its underside is white or cream. Its mouth turns down like a frown.

Length: Usually 5.6 feet (1.7 m)

Weight: Up to 40 pounds (18 kg)

Behavior

The whitetip reef shark feeds on small fish, eels, octopuses, and crabs. It hunts for food at night and rests during the day. Many sharks need to swim in order to breathe. As they swim, water moves through their mouths and pushes oxygen through their gills. But the whitetip reef shark can pull water through its gills while resting. Unlike many sharks, it can stop swimming and not risk dying.

Range

Whitetip reef sharks are found near Australia and South Africa. They swim in the Red Sea. They are also found near Costa Rica.

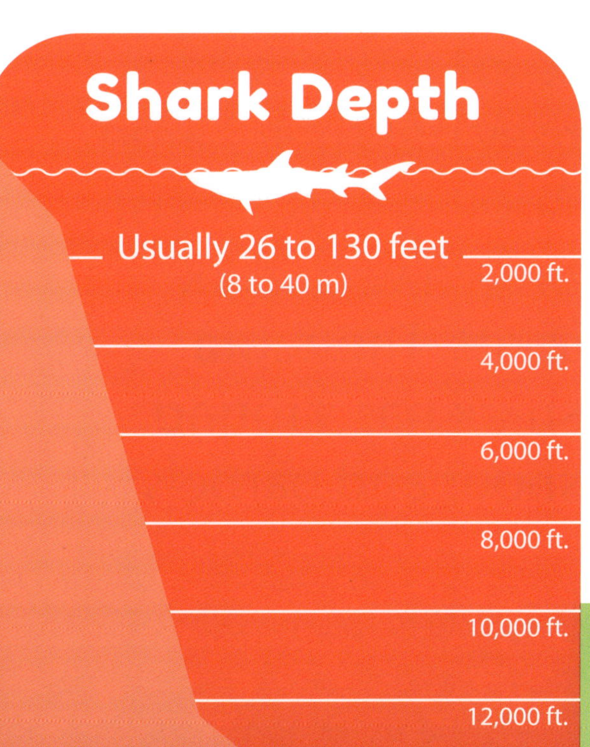

ZEBRA SHARK

(*Stegostoma fasciatum*)

Young zebra sharks have stripes.

Appearance

Young zebra sharks are black and white. They have stripes. This is how they get their name. Adults are yellowish brown with dark spots. The zebra shark has a round snout and barbels.

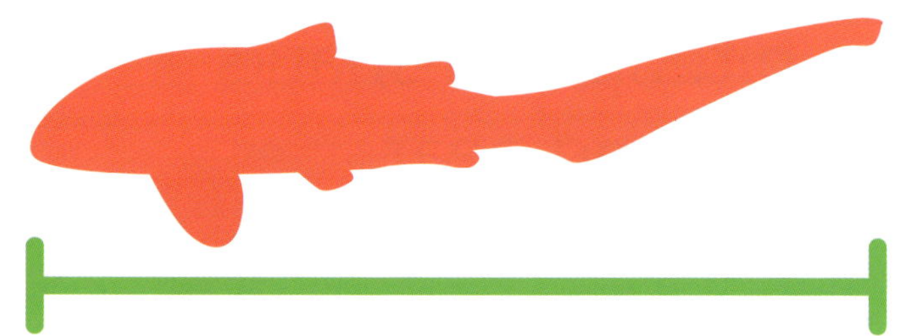

Length: Up to 11 feet (3.5 m)

Weight: 35 to 44 pounds (16 to 20 kg)

Adult zebra sharks have spots.

Behavior

Zebra sharks live in areas where the water is warm. They stay near the sandy bottom. They also swim near coral reefs and rock reefs. Zebra sharks hunt for food at night. They eat mollusks, fish, and crustaceans.

Range

Zebra sharks are found in the western Pacific Ocean. They also live in the Indian Ocean and the Red Sea. They swim along the coast.

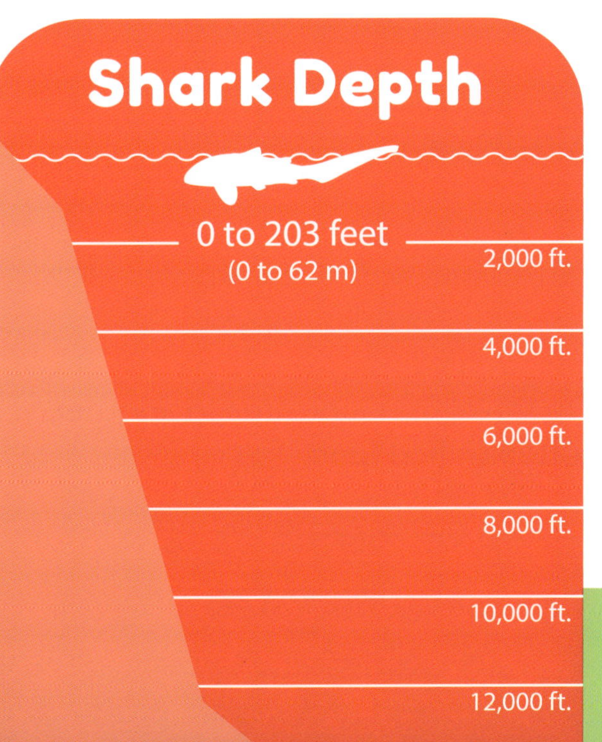

GLOSSARY

barbel
A whisker-like growth on a fish's lip.

blunt
Having a shape that is rounded, not sharp.

camouflage
The natural coloring of an animal that allows it to hide in its environment.

cartilage
Strong, flexible tissue in the skeleton of some animals. Human ears have cartilage.

crustacean
A class of sea animals including lobsters, shrimp, and crabs.

dorsal
On the back of an animal.

invertebrate
An animal with no backbone.

migrate
To travel from one area to another, often to find food.

mollusk
A class of invertebrates including snails, clams, and octopuses.

plankton
A small animal or plant that floats in the ocean.

prey
An animal that is hunted by other animals.

ray
A fish with a cartilage skeleton, wing-like fins, and a thin tail.

serrated
Jagged along the edges, like a saw.

skate
A fish in the ray family with a flat, diamond-shaped body.

species
A group of living things that have similar characteristics.

vertebrate
An animal with a backbone.

TO LEARN MORE

More Books to Read

Boyer, Crispin. *So Cool! Sharks*. National Geographic Kids, 2019.

McGuire, David. *Sharks for Kids: A Junior Scientist's Guide to Great Whites, Hammerheads, and Other Sharks in the Sea*. Rockridge, 2020.

Murray, Julie. *Fun Facts about Sharks*. Abdo, 2021.

Online Resources

To learn more about sharks, please visit **abdobooklinks.com** or scan this QR code. These links are routinely monitored and updated to provide the most current information available.

INDEX

PHOTO CREDITS

Cover Photos: Alessandro De Maddalena/Shutterstock, front (great white); Shutterstock, front (great hammerhead), front (zebra shark), back (water splash); Photo Junction/Shutterstock, front (underwater background); Eric Isselee/Shutterstock, back (shark)

Interior Photos: Shutterstock, 1, 3, 11, 22, 22–23 (silhouette), 23, 24, 28–29, 32, 46–47 (silhouette), 48–49 (silhouette), 52, 52–53 (silhouette), 56–57 (silhouette), 63, 64, 66–67 (silhouette), 70–71 (silhouette), 73, 74–75 (silhouette), 86–87 (silhouette), 87, 90–91 (silhouette), 97, 100–101 (silhouette), 106–107 (silhouette), 110, 112, 112–113 (silhouette), 113, 114–115 (silhouette), 116–117 (silhouette), 117, 124–125 (silhouette); Lukas Walter/Shutterstock, 5; Auscape/Universal Images Group/Getty Images, 6, 124; Tom Fricker Design/Shutterstock, 7 (silhouette), 8–9 (silhouette), 10–11 (silhouette), 13 (silhouette), 14–15 (silhouette), 16–17 (silhouette), 18–19 (silhouette), 20–21 (silhouette), 24–25 (silhouette), 26–27 (silhouette), 28–29 (silhouette), 36–37 (silhouette), 40–41 (silhouette), 42–43 (silhouette), 54–55 (silhouette), 62–63 (silhouette), 68–69 (silhouette), 72–73 (silhouette), 94–95 (silhouette), 98–99 (silhouette), 102–103 (silhouette), 120–121 (silhouette); Martin Prochazkacz/Shutterstock, 8, 27, 53, 96; Rebecca Belleni Photography/iStockphoto, 9; Jeff Rotman/Science Source, 10; Lagunatic Photo/iStockphoto, 12; Eric Isselee/Shutterstock, 14–15; Willyam Bradberry/Shutterstock, 15; Stefan Pircher/Shutterstock Images, 16, 26; Aleksandr Golubev/iStockphoto, 17; Alessandro De Maddalena/Shutterstock, 18–19; Pommeyrol Vincent/Shutterstock, 19; Eric Cheng/Blue Planet Archive, 20, 21; Charlotte Bleijenberg/Shutterstock, 25; iStockphoto, 29, 62–63, 72, 100, 104, 115, 119; Doug Perrine/Blue Planet Archive, 30–31, 31, 38, 57, 68–69, 82, 93, 106, 107; Mansiliya Yury/Shutterstock, 30–31 (silhouette), 50–51 (silhouette), 60–61 (silhouette), 80–81 (silhouette), 118–119 (silhouette); Amadeu Blasco/Shutterstock, 32–33 (silhouette), 34–35 (silhouette), 38–39 (silhouette), 76–77 (silhouette), 78–79 (silhouette), 82–83 (silhouette), 84–85 (silhouette), 88–89 (silhouette), 104–105 (silhouette); D. R. Schrichte/Blue Planet Archive, 33, 61, 89; Luis Miguel Estevez/Shutterstock, 34, 35; Saul Gonor/Blue Planet Archive, 36, 56; Marty Snyderman/Blue Planet Archive, 37; The Natural History Museum of London/Science Source, 39; Miguel Lopez Laguna/Shutterstock, 40; Michael Leonard/Blue Planet Archive, 41; Jeff Milisen/Blue Planet Archive, 42; Blue Planet Archive, 43; Ian Scott/Shutterstock, 44–45; Sky Pics Studio/Shutterstock, 44–45 (silhouette), 58–59 (silhouette), 64–65 (silhouette), 92–93 (silhouette), 96–97 (silhouette), 108–109 (silhouette), 110–111 (silhouette), 122–123 (silhouette); Michael Aw/Blue Planet Archive, 45; Kelvin Aitken/VW Pics/AP Images, 46; Gwen Lowe/Blue Planet Archive, 47; David Shen/Blue Planet Archive, 48; Makoto Hirose/E Photo/Blue Planet Archive, 49; Ute Niemann/iStockphoto, 50–51; Marco Zucchini/iStockphoto, 51; Andrea Izzotti/Shutterstock, 54–55; Sergey Uryadnikov/Shutterstock, 55; Andy Murch/Blue Planet Archive, 58–59, 59, 75, 77, 79, 83, 85; Richard Herrmann/Blue Planet Archive, 60–61; R. Maximiliane/Shutterstock, 65; Bruce Rasner/Blue Planet Archive, 66–67, 67; Andre Seale/Blue Planet Archive, 69, 116–117; Shane Gross/Shutterstock, 70; Rainer von Brandis/iStockphoto, 71; Ethan Daniels/Blue Planet Archive, 74; John Muhilly/Blue Planet Archive, 76; Doug Perrine/Alamy, 78–79; Dirk van der Heide/Shutterstock, 80; Holly Harry/Shutterstock, 81; Warren Metcalf/Shutterstock, 84–85; Tomas Kotouc/Shutterstock, 86, 94; Vladimir Wrangel/Shutterstock, 88; Joe Dordo Brnobic/Shutterstock, 90; Nicolas SB/Shutterstock, 91; Michael Zeigler/iStockphoto, 92; Gilberto Villasana/iStockphoto, 95; Ethan Daniels/Shutterstock, 98; Benny Marty/Shutterstock, 99; Prisma Bildagentur/Dukas/Universal Images Group/Getty Images, 101; Jeff Rotman/Blue Planet Archive, 102; Luis Javier Sandoval/VW Pics/Universal Images Group/Getty Images, 103; Espen Rekdal/Blue Planet Archive, 105; C & M Fallows/Blue Planet Archive, 108; Gerald Robert Fischer/Shutterstock, 114; Pete's Photography/iStockphoto, 118; David B. Fleetham/Blue Planet Archive, 120; Phillip Colla/Blue Planet Archive, 121; Leonardo Gonzalez/Shutterstock, 122; Rudmer Zwerver/Shutterstock, 123; Richard Whitcombe/Shutterstock, 125